The
SPRING
of
NATIONS

The
SPRING
of
NATIONS

Churches in the Rebirth of Central and Eastern Europe

J. MARTIN BAILEY

Friendship Press • New York

Copyright © 1991 by Friendship Press

Editorial Offices:
475 Riverside Drive, New York, NY 10115

Distribution Offices:
P.O. Box 37844, Cincinnati, OH 45222-0844

Manufactured in the United States of America

Library of Congress Cataloging-in-Publication Data

Bailey, J. Martin, 1929-
  The spring of nations : churches in the rebirth of Central and Eastern
Europe / by J. Martin Bailey.
      p.   cm.
  Includes index.
  ISBN 0-377-00224-0
  1. Christianity—Europe, Eastern. 2. Europe, Eastern—Church
history. 3. Communism and Christianity—Europe, Eastern.
4. Europe, Eastern—Politics and government—1945-1989. 5. Europe,
Eastern—Politics and government—1989-   I. Title.
BR738.6.B33 1991
274.3'0828—dc20
                                                              91-7300
                                                                CIP

For Jimmy:

a world without walls

I am most grateful for the assistance of Barbara G. Green, Kenneth R. Zibell, Michael F. Möller, Robert C. Lodwick, Dwain Epps, and Theodore H. Erickson, all of whom read the manuscript in its initial stages and offered helpful advice. They are, of course, in no way responsible for the final version.

Contents

Part III
HOPES AND FEARS

Preface

It is impossible without Christ to understand the history of the Polish nation.

> — Pope John Paul II, June 2, 1979,
> on the occasion of his first visit
> to Poland after his election as pope

The homecoming of "the Polish pope" was as significant and far-reaching as it was dramatic and emotional. Standing beneath an enormous fifty-foot cross erected in Warsaw's Victory Square, the son of working-class Poles flatly challenged the Communist government officials who were determined to create an atheistic state. "If we seek to view Poland without Christ and Christianity," he told the crowd and a national television audience, "we lay ourselves open to a substantial misunderstanding. We no longer understand ourselves."

The thesis of this little book is a paraphrase of those words of John Paul II: It is impossible without Christianity and the church to understand the historic events of 1989–90 that have changed the face of Central and Eastern Europe and the self-understanding of nearly all peoples.

During the fall and winter of 1989 the gales of change blew — no, pounded — across Europe. Governments toppled. The seemingly impenetrable Wall became a dance stage before it was pushed aside by men and women who were at once joyful in their new-found freedom and unbelieving when they recognized their own power. The ideology that had controlled Central and Eastern Europe since the end of World War II was discredited, even in the eyes of many of its protagonists. And, more important, in an essentially peaceful transition the stereotypes of power were blown out like the miniature candles on a birthday cake.

The events claimed the headlines for months; few news stories were ever so thoroughly covered. (Some analysts believe that the instantaneous and worldwide coverage of this news contributed to the movement itself.) Still, the television and print journalists failed to describe thoroughly one recurring and central theme as the story evolved. There were, to be sure, references to heroic pastors. Television audiences caught glimpses of candle-lit worship services. Some fleeting attention was given to the urgent prayers that the revolution be kept nonviolent. *Time* magazine reported that behind the opposition movement in Eastern Germany was "an amorphous collection of mild-mannered pastors, artists and writers. The movement's strength is its links to the Protestant church, attended by more than 40 percent of East German citizens."

Nevertheless, the central and formative role of the churches in the democracy movement in Central and Eastern Europe was never adequately reported. As this book seeks to show, many of those who were close to the eye of the whirlwind acknowledged the role of the churches. But the media, typically, focused on politicians and on celebrities, on chanting crowds and on bulldozers and wire-cutters. The news was engrossing. History was being made. But *how* history was made was never fully reported. I believe that the gale-force winds were the breath of God's Spirit.

One person who has recognized the formative role of the churches in these changes is Representative Douglas K. Bereuter of Nebraska, who is a member of the House Foreign Affairs Committee. He says, unequivocally, that "it is impossible to talk about foreign policy in Eastern Europe without talking about what the religious institutions are doing there." He believes that some of the groundwork for the leadership provided by the churches was laid as early as 1983 during the celebrations in the German Democratic Republic of the five hundredth anniversary of the birth of Martin Luther.[1] He credits the clergy and laity who, "by their deeds and by their words, are acting as a moral beacon to a new era for their countries and the world." He notes with expectation that the "new governments in Eastern Europe will have unprecedented access to moral and spiritual leadership."

This book has been compiled from many testimonies. It began to take shape during the visit of an official delegation from the National Council of the Churches of Christ in the U.S.A. to counterpart ecumenical agencies in Poland and Hungary. It was on October 14, 1989 — a bright fall day in Warsaw — when Prime Bishop Tadeusz R. Majewski of the Polish Catholic Church greeted us on behalf of his country's ecumenical council. We were anticipating conversations with Solidarity leaders who now were in the seats of government, and we looked forward to days in Budapest where remarkable changes also had begun to take place. At his diocesan office, Bishop Majewski said, so simply that we could almost have missed it, "Welcome to autumn in Poland — the spring of nations."

Our interviews with religious and political leaders in both countries helped me begin to understand how deeply the churches were involved in the momentous events. We talked with pastors, with lay women and lay men, with youth, with legislators and teachers, with taxi drivers and people on the street. With a kind of evangelical zeal all we met seemed eager to tell their stories. We felt fortu-

---

[1] Others, including Barbara Green, who worked with the German churches from 1977 to 1981, believe that the foundations were laid in the church-state accords signed in 1978. These are described in detail below; see p. 43.

nate to share in some small measure the euphoria and the anxiety that always seemed mixed in equal proportions. In Warsaw, for example, Andreij Wielowieyski, the new vice president of the Senate, spoke at length of his country's desperate economic morass. His tone was sober, yet confidently determined. We arrived in Budapest on the very day that workers began taking the red stars from the tops of government buildings. The day we left, Imre Pozsgay, the minister of state who had received us graciously, proclaimed that the name of the country henceforth would be the Republic of Hungary. Then and there I began collecting the stories. I talked with women and men who helped make history and with eyewitnesses. I clipped newspapers and magazines. I corresponded with people who themselves had experienced the events. The histories that I began devouring suddenly described a living reality.

As dramatic and numerous as these reports are, I recognize their inadequacy. This book is not a definitive narrative. It certainly is not a history of the period. It is but a collection of reports that might assist some future historian. I will be satisfied if it helps Christians see how the church and the faith made a difference in desperate situations.

I also recognize some of the dangers inherent in publishing these stories. Recorded as they are so soon after the events, they too easily may reflect the excitement of a headlong movement. Many of the people I quote know only too well the serious and complex problems that they face. But, happily, they are now dealing with the economic and social realities themselves, rather than watching someone else struggle clumsily with neither popular support nor corrective criticism. And, even more happily, they are seeking their own answers without having to accept "solutions" imposed from outside.

I have tried to avoid Western chauvinism, for I do not believe that answers can be exported any more successfully from North America to Central and Eastern Europe than they could be imposed effectively from the Soviet Union. While we were in Poland, a very enthusiastic deputy minister of education explained to me how the new government intended to revise the nation's entire educational system. The plan, already being implemented, called for a research team to visit West Germany, England and the United States to find a model to adopt. I understand the sense of urgency that drives that effort, but I have serious doubts that a single effective model can be located and adopted. Adapted? Perhaps. I warned my new friend about some of the pitfalls of the U.S. educational system. I trust that educators with greater competence than I also offered the counsel of caution. Yet in other spheres, such as economics and business, there is evidence that Western capitalism may be exported by persons with more confidence in their own abilities than understanding of the problems of other cultures. Unfortunately even in religion, some North Americans are so eager to help that as they provide assistance they are zealously broadcasting an all-too-American form of religious expression.

There is also a danger that these reports will be misread. I do not join the chorus of those who gleefully are singing, "We knew your system was wrong; we could have told you it would fail." Nor do I want these stories to contribute to any pious self-satisfaction. As Robert Bellah contends, "The real temptation for America is triumphalism, which leads to the feeling that *they* have failed and *we* have won." We, in what some people call the Free West, have much to learn from the experiences of those who live in Central or Eastern Europe. Their bitter suffering during the long winter of the Cold War cannot be overestimated. It will take generations for the psychological and ecological scars to heal. But that suffering has forged strength as well, and in the often hostile circumstances, new indigenous models have been tested and refined. Our own learnings from their years of agony will begin when we confess that Western insensitivities as well as our drive for power often contributed to the problem rather than helped to provide a solution. Further, if we are to learn from their experience we need to be prepared to reflect objectively on the circumstances in which Western assumptions have been misguided and on the situations in which Eastern values are still seen as desirable. With Bellah, I hope that we can acknowledge the culpability that capitalists and communists share — "the pervasive materialism that pervades both our cultures." Surely we who live in North America need to acknowledge that the freedoms we enjoy are relative — and fragile.

Many of the news reports during the late fall of 1989 and the winter of 1990 described what was happening as the "rebirth of democracy." That was a considerable overstatement. Most of the nations described have had virtually no history of democracy. Earlier attempts were short lived and those who are forging a new society today are too young to have had any personal experience with freedom. They have had few opportunities to develop the skills needed for self-government except in such organizations as churches and labor movements. Many of the churches are themselves hierarchical in polity, and one criticism of Lech Wałęsa's leadership of the Solidarity trade union was that too often he acted on his own. One of the great dangers to the stability of the nations formerly under Communist control, therefore, is this lack of experience and the absence of an established political infrastructure. As developments in places like Czechoslovakia and Romania continue to unfold, it will be instructive to watch how the churches nurture and support new leaders.

This modest book, then, is an effort to report on the role of the churches not only in tearing down a Wall but also in building up a new society. Both efforts are rooted in faith. Both are empowered by faithfulness. If, as I have asserted, there is evidence of God's Spirit at work, there is special reason for gratitude.

INTRODUCTION

Piety and Nationhood

Our first president [Tomáš Masaryk] wrote: "Jesus not Caesar." Today this idea again came to life in us. I dare say that perhaps we have a possibility of spreading it further on and thus introducing a new element to European and world policy.... Masaryk based his policy on morality.... Let's teach both ourselves and the others that policy need not be only the art of the possible, especially if we mean with this the art of speculations, calculations, intrigues, secret agreements and pragmatic maneuvering, but that it can be, also, the art of the impossible, namely the art to do both ourselves and the world better. We are a small country, nevertheless in spite of this we used to be at the spiritual crossroads of Europe. Why couldn't we become it again? Wouldn't it be another contribution, with which we could pay back help to the others?

— Václav Havel, on the occasion of
his inaugural address as president of the
Republic of Czechoslovakia, January 1, 1990

Christian piety is the warp on which the tapestry of many Central and Eastern European nations is woven.

Autocratic rulers in earlier generations and again during the last half of the twentieth century failed to understand that the spiritual roots of a nation are tangible — as real and as essential as a pantry full of food. The faith of the people is never far below the surface, though it may

15

be spoken of casually. Together with their national and ethnic identities, the relatively unsophisticated religious beliefs of millions of people made it impossible for Marxism (especially when it was imposed from the outside) to win the loyalty of the masses. More than any other factor — certainly more than economic determinism — the expression of religious convictions led to the failure of the Communist experiment in Central and Eastern Europe.

From Germany and Czechoslovakia eastward, the religious expression of the people varied greatly. In the former German Democratic Republic, the strong threads for the tapestry were twisted and dyed during and after the Protestant Reformation of the sixteenth century. Of these, the Lutheran strands are the most numerous, although within the Evangelical Church of the Union there is a significant Reformed heritage as well. Theirs is a rich biblical tradition that understands that Christians are called upon to act as well as to worship.

Roman Catholicism dominates Poland, although the closer one gets to the Soviet border in the East the greater the influence of Eastern Orthodoxy. Even in Catholic parishes and in centers of pilgrimage like Czestochowa, Eastern piety is noticeable. The preeminent example of this is the icon of the "black Madonna" at the Monastery of Jasna Gora. Private devotion, as well as public worship, is highly valued; priests, bishops and the pope enjoy high credibility. The church and its rites are accepted by the people as a natural part of daily life.

Roman Catholic and Reformed traditions blend in different ways in Czechoslovakia and Hungary. In the former, popular attitudes concerning social justice derive from the heroic figure of Jan Hus, a reformer who lived and died a century before Martin Luther. In Hungary, the firm and sometimes painfully decisive words of John Calvin continue to echo in a society in which the church's interest in education has played a prominent role. In both Hungary and Czechoslovakia, the Roman Church is numerically stronger than Protestant and Orthodox churches; in neither country, however, does it overshadow the other religious communities as it does in Poland. The reformed tradition in both countries encourages serious theological discourse.

The Eastern Orthodox faith clearly is the strongest religious expression in Romania, though significant groups of Hungarians and other minorities have maintained their own religious practices. The Orthodox emphasis on liturgy and frequent attendance at worship remains central to the people's lives.

In addition, Central and Eastern Europe include many ethnic groups, with regional and national traditions and practices that run very deep. The ethnic histories and identities of many communities often lead to local pride and sometimes to partisan rivalries. These rivalries and prejudices too frequently have led to violence and even have triggered warfare. Many persons are concerned that the sudden power vacuum in that region has created new opportunities for intergroup strife.

As is usually the case, Christian piety has developed ethnic overtones that, with the passage of time, become difficult to separate from essential Christian practice. A major factor in the spread of Christianity has been its ability to accommodate and even to absorb some of these regional patterns. Generally, this is wholesome: it is the Word becoming flesh in new surroundings. Unfortunately, however, it has also sometimes taken on a patina of nationalism. In the long history of Central and Eastern Europe, that happened from time to time. During the turbulent period that followed the Reformation, the churches that reflected and preserved national identities were sometimes Protestant, sometimes Catholic.

Significantly, during the six decades that included World War II and the division of Europe, the churches provided a corporate memory that preserved and transmitted ethnic and national identities. One only needs to look at Poland to observe the importance of that fact. That nation provided a battleground for Europe's giants. In the twentieth century there were concerted efforts, first by the Nazis and later by the Soviets, to alter the self-perceptions of the Polish people. Neither succeeded, because the memory of faith was stronger than the skill and even the military might that the Nazis and Soviets assembled. The church, with its colorful traditions, had been part of the people's lives for generations. Similarly in Romania, Nicolae Ceausescu tried consciously to alter the allegiance of the Hungarian minority population. That effort also failed because the Christian community in Hungarian-speaking regions of Romania had remained, in fact, a Hungarian community.

National or ethnic identities thus have been strengthened by a generally subtle relationship to what is perceived to be divine intervention or God's own will for the people. Mystical connections, as when Our Lady of Czestochowa is revered as the Queen of Poland, take root in a nation's psyche and cannot be expunged by force. But such an implied relationship to the will of God can be problematic, as well. Adolf Hitler and others sought to subvert the church and its symbols. Some historians have tried to show that one possible reading of Lutheran theology encouraged — or at least failed to halt — the rise of Nazism. The formation of an official Reich Church provides a dramatic example of the political abuse of religious institutions, an example that can be matched — less dramatically, perhaps — in many other societies.

The twentieth century has brought a number of moderating influences to the concept of a *Volkskirche* — an ethnocentric, nationalist or people's church — in the countries of Central and Eastern Europe. Although the ties between the churches and cultural or national identities are very strong, several other very important factors are now involved. Societies increasingly are becoming secular, and even where there is a large nominal church membership or a commonly accepted affirmation of belief, the close relation of the church to the state can no longer be assumed. There is now open debate about whether the church and state should be separated. In Eastern and Central Europe, one legacy of the Marxist period is that freedom to believe or not to believe is generally accepted as a value to be protected.

Another contemporary factor is the growing awareness that the church is supranational and multidimensional. The ecumenical movement has provided both a positive experience and a theological rationale that looks beyond the parochial and national to an international or universal good. Both a better understanding of the principles of church unity and recent initiatives in support of peace, justice and the protection of the environment have led churches in Central and Eastern Europe and around the world to view their roles quite differently from the way they did before World War II. Observing people now commonly are aware that the church has made major contributions to the quality of their lives. This is especially true in relation to the world church's advocacy for human rights and to the way the church functions as a servant to those in need. Because so many persons, including national leaders, are aware that the church has functioned well during recent years, many will be ready to listen to critical analysis as well as specific recommendations from prophetic voices. In some areas, however, there are serious reservations rooted in suspicions that some churches and church leaders worked too closely with state officials.

It is useful to recognize that throughout the region there is a dynamic tension between the historic relationships of the church to regional or national cultures on the one hand and the experience of a worldwide religious community that assists and protects the aspirations of people on the other. It was within that tension that the churches of Poland, Hungary, East Germany, Czechoslovakia and Romania played significant roles during the

democracy movement of 1989–90. It will be within that
tension that the churches and their leaders must function
as they seek now to serve under changed and changing
circumstances.

Part I

Behind the Curtain

*If God's free grace is the ultimate reality in the world,
nothing can separate us from the love of God.*

— Albrecht Schönherr, bishop of Berlin-
Brandenburg, urging the churches to a faithful
witness within the totalitarian and atheistic society
of the German Democratic Republic, March 1978

CHAPTER ONE

Contacts in Isolation

The oppression that the Christians of Central and Eastern Europe experienced in the nearly five decades since the end of World War II came in waves of severity and was more directly expressed in some countries than in others. In most places their churches were repressed; some were effectively forced underground. Among the enormous burdens that these Christians shared with others in their nations was enforced isolation; most persons were denied the right to go abroad. Husbands and wives almost never were permitted to travel together except possibly to other Communist countries. Many persons were intimidated by the likelihood that mail from another country would be opened and read before delivery.

The ugly Wall that bisected Berlin became the symbol of what Winston Churchill described as an Iron Curtain as early as 1946. But those who built the Wall never were able to sever the ties that bound Christians to one another. The Wall was, nevertheless, an affront to the dignity and a constriction on the aspirations of all who felt its impact. Those on the eastern side suffered most, but its harsh reality also was known in the West and throughout the world. Families were divided. A nation was carved in two. And the unity of the church was impaired.

Yet even where they lived with some form of daily repression, the churches for the most part were faithful to the gospel. Often this faithfulness required individuals to take considerable risks and to make significant sacrifices. In some instances religious institutions learned to accommodate external pressures while preserving the ministry of word and sacrament.

In most places, the educational efforts and social service witness of the churches were eliminated. The official philosophy of the Communist leaders was atheism, which was taught in the schools and insinuated in various ways into cultures that earlier had reflected a Christian heritage intricately interwoven with their national histories. As in the Soviet Union, alternatives were provided for Christian festivals and rites of passage. Marriages, for example, were performed with state-centered rituals or overt atheistic messages. Not long after the Communists came to power in East Germany they sought to replace confirmation with *Jugendweihe*, or "youth dedication," a coming-of-age ceremony in which youth were expected to swear allegiance to the state. The education of youth was regarded by the state as of very high priority. In the German Democratic Republic secondary school pupils who were involved in the church frequently were expelled from school, sometimes on the accusation of being agents of the United States Central Intelligence Agency or West German intelligence organizations.

Throughout Central and Eastern Europe secular trends, also evident in Western nations, enjoyed official sponsorship. Not only were church-sponsored schools nationalized but Christian education generally was limited to the home; even there training in the faith was discouraged. Higher education often was unavailable to believers; employment opportunities were limited or denied. Many not-so-subtle means were used by the state to discourage church attendance and religious practice. Nevertheless, the long history of the Christian church was repeated: martyrdom and repression led again to courageous expressions of faithfulness.

The socialist governments assumed that various forms of social service (some of which had been pioneered by the churches) were now the exclusive province and obligation of the state. In a classless society, there could be no poverty and the needs of all persons had to be met. Where such services were effective and universal, Christians sometimes applauded. The phrase "socialism with a human face" was used to describe an ideal situation in which health care, education and other services were available to all who needed them within a planned and increasingly open society. These "social rights" were considered, even by some theologians, to be at least as important as, if not more significant than, individual freedoms like the right to own property, to communicate openly or to travel across international frontiers. That judgment is still held by some today.

Communication with Christians in other parts of the world was restricted during much of the period. Until recently, personal contact was limited to those who ventured through the wall of separation for short periods and to prudent and infrequent conversations. A major exception was the participation of East and Central European church leaders in peace consultations and international religious activities. For Protestants and Orthodox these included meetings of the World Council of Churches and of the Conference of European Churches. For Roman Catholics, they consisted primarily of conversations and ecclesiastical events at the Vatican.

Especially during the so-called Stalinist period, and when the pressures on the churches were especially severe, many skeptical Western Christians assumed that in places like East Germany, Czechoslovakia, Hungary and Poland the churches had been forced to accommodate the Communist leaders. It appeared that some leaders uncritically accepted and often echoed Soviet foreign policy. The real heroes, according to some Western observers, were those who were executed, imprisoned or exiled for their faith.

It is now evident that the faithfulness of church members, pastors, theologians and church officials was both steady and demonstrable, although since January 1990 several leaders have been criticized or replaced because they had earlier supported government policies. It is clear, however, that the essential integrity of the church, expressed in a wide variety of ways, contributed significantly to the democracy movement of 1989.

"You Helped Us Look over the Border"

One way that the faithfulness of the church was encouraged and expressed was through contacts with Christians from countries in the West and in the Third World. These conversations, especially when levels of trust and understanding had been developed, were valued by Christians in both East and West.

Certainly one of the most extensive networks of relationships existed between church people in the former German Democratic Republic and their counterparts in the West. Relationships with friends, family and fellow Christians in the Federal Republic of Germany were of a special character and importance. For example, nearly every one of the two hundred or so East German United Methodist Churches developed a church-to-church relationship with a West German Methodist congregation. There were an estimated twenty-five thousand Methodists in the GDR and approximately twice that number in the Federal Republic. The two bishops, Walter Klaiber in the West and Rüdiger Minor in the East, were careful to avoid letting the Western congregations be "rich uncles." Rather, they looked for ways in which Methodists in the two parts of Germany could learn from one another. The same was true among Lutheran and United churches on an even larger scale.

The Federation of Evangelical Churches in the GDR was created in 1969 by East German Christians when their government required a formal break with the West German church. Even then, however, the church made it clear that a spiritual unity would continue with its counterpart on the other side of the Wall. Regular contacts were maintained with the Evangelical Church Federation in West Germany (EKD).

The Evangelical Church of the Union (EKU) had synods in each of the two German states. It developed procedures for regular, almost constant contact between the two synods. The ecumenical officer of the EKU/West, Reinhard Groscurth, made several trips to the GDR each week to meet with colleagues in the EKU/East, especially with Christa Grengel, his counterpart. The two synods regularly took similar or identical actions, seeking to function as normally as possible.

The Evangelical Church of the Union also has a special partnership with the United Church of Christ in the United States, a relationship called *Kirchengemeinschaft*, full church communion, negotiated at the highest levels of the churches. Since 1981 when the partnership was celebrated during the United Church General Synod, hundreds of pastors and lay persons have been able to visit in one another's churches and homes; theologians have pursued joint studies on such issues as peace and human rights as well as liturgy and doctrine; friendships approaching familial ties have developed. Enormous energy has been expended in cultivating and maintaining those relationships, always out of a conviction that the unity given by Christ to the church needed to be affirmed, celebrated and strengthened. This partnership will certainly continue and be extended in the new situation.

In several cases regional organizations (conferences,

associations, districts, synods) have expressed this partnership through correspondence and joint events. Grassroots
contacts, which have been going on for twenty-five years,
now take the form of an annual exchange during which
there are meetings with church leaders and visits in
congregations. On alternate years a delegation of eight persons from the United Church of Christ, four from each of
two conferences, spends a month with the EKU in East
and West Germany.

Immanuel Congregational United Church of Christ in
Hartford, Connecticut, has been involved in a particularly significant partnership relationship that also includes
a British congregation, churches in both East and West
Germany, and one in Czechoslovakia. The pastor of the
congregation in Dessau in June 1990 described how important that partnership had been for his congregation in
what was then the German Democratic Republic. "There
was a border between East and West," Wolfgang Steckel
wrote to the Rev. Richard B. Griffis, pastor of the Hartford church. "What a border! A high Wall, barbed wire,
mines, a strip of death. But you crossed the border. We in
Dessau were very thankful for your courage. It was very
good for us to see that we are not forgotten, to see that
there are Christians who are willing to bear our burden, to
live under an unloved, oppressive government. Your visits
helped us to see over the border, which seemed to us so
definitive."

Over nearly twenty years the five congregations have
held seven international partnership conferences that engage lay persons and clergy in substantial numbers from
each of the five churches. The 1989 conference was held
at the Petruskirche (St. Peter's Church) in Dessau from
July 28 to August 7. Aware of the strains in their society
and of probable bureaucratic delays, the national church
leaders urged that a mini-meeting be held. The congregation persisted, however, and visas for the guests eventually
were issued. Nearly one hundred persons participated,

with the theme "Christians Today with Responsibility for Tomorrow."

A lay leader in the Petruskirche, Lothar Biener, wrote to the other churches in January 1990 saying that the event was "for us a grand experience. The wonderful atmosphere of these ten days, the interesting talks and experiences together was the greatest reward for all who had prepared and for those who worked in the background. From the very first minute, during the whole course, we looked into beaming faces. With these faces we can be credible in proclaiming the Good News." The same letter included a congratulatory message sent to the partner Evangelical Church of Czech Brethren congregation in Ostrava, Czechoslovakia, "in the achievement of a nonviolent revolution in their country, and whom we wish much success in the building of democracy."

Such human contact is extraordinarily important. As early as 1987 the Federation of Evangelical Churches in the GDR was able to persuade the government to provide residency permits for Gratia and Steven Johns-Boehme, from the United States, the first ecumenical co-workers to live in the GDR. For two and a half years they served liaison roles, working both with Lutheran and United congregations, and sharing intensively in the life and witness of the church within that socialist society. Reinhard Groscurth told a special convocation at Eden Theological Seminary in St. Louis early in 1990 how deeply moved East German Christians were when they received a letter during the fall of 1989 from a group of Eden students assuring their German friends of intercessory prayers and of Christian solidarity. He also quoted his cousin, a pastor in Stendal: "When the dark clouds of desperation came closer to the land and to the people, suddenly a phone call from the Netherlands: 'We remember you.' Only that one sentence. But words which made the night bright." Eden Seminary, related to the United Church of Christ, presented honorary degrees in 1990 to both Groscurth and Grengel, as it had in 1936 to three German pastors, Gerhard Jacobi, Otto Dibelius and Martin Niemöller, each of whom was then involved in the Confessing Church's opposition to Hitler.

Participation in the worldwide ecumenical fellowship has created deep bonds of support and provided the courage for many Christians to act. The EKU–United Church of Christ partnership has dealt substantively with the broader ecumenical research on "Justice, Peace and the Integrity of Creation." That theme of a World Council of Churches conference in Seoul, Korea, also was the topic of a major pan-European Ecumenical Assembly held May 15–21, 1989, in Basel, Switzerland. Sponsored jointly by the Conference of European Churches and the Roman Catholic Council of European Bishops' Conferences, the assembly candidly assessed threats to justice, to peace and to the environment in the European context. Church leaders from the socialist nations had been among the first to encourage international discussions on that subject that to them was of more than academic interest.

Coming as it did on the eve of the dramatic events in Central and Eastern Europe, the Basel assembly offered an opportunity for both formal and informal conversations on what had become the central issues facing their nations. Preparatory studies among the churches of most European nations meant that the topics were being considered both within a theological and ethical framework and in terms of a concrete assessment of present circumstances. In the German Democratic Republic, for example, the "Conciliar Process for Justice, Peace and the Integrity of the Creation," was welcomed because it provided an opportunity to discuss domestic issues under church auspices. The five hundred delegates at the assembly in Basel acknowledged, for example, that "human rights are being violated on a massive scale. This is true for economic, social, cultural and religious rights, as well as civil and political rights."

This ecumenical and international assembly overwhelmingly adopted a final report that, among other things, called for "special attention to the democratic reforms in the Soviet Union and other East European countries." The final report also looked inward, affirming that

Today conversion to God means a commitment to seeking ways

- out of the divisions between rich and poor, between powerful and powerless,

- out of structures which cause hunger, deprivation and death,

- out of the unemployment of millions of people,

- out of a world in which human rights are violated and where people are tortured and isolated,

- out of a way of life in which moral and ethical values are undermined or even cast aside,

into a society where people have equal rights and live together in solidarity.

Such formal and informal ecumenical conversations provided an immensely important human bridge across political divisions. Western European Christians discovered insights from their colleagues living in Poland, Hungary, Czechoslovakia and the German Democratic Republic. Church leaders from Central and Eastern Europe, as well as the members of congregations and even nonparticipants in the organizational life of the churches, found solidarity and encouragement from the contacts. It is impossible to overestimate the significance of this ecumenical dialogue in relation to the movements that culminated in the fall and winter of 1989.

The People of Poland, Their Priests and Their Pope

The isolation that Central and Eastern Europe experienced during the Communist period followed the brutal years of World War II. Limitations on travel and correspondence actually began in 1939. This isolation is illustrated in the early life of Karol Wojtyła, who became Pope John Paul II.

When the Nazis invaded Poland the universities were closed and students were forced to work. Hitler's instructions to the commandant for the area around Kraków, where Karol lived, were clear: "The Poles are born for low labor.... The standard of living must be kept low. The priests will preach what we want them to preach. If any priest acts differently, we will make short work of him. The task of priests is to keep the Poles quiet, stupid and dull-witted."

When the universities were closed Karol first worked in a stone quarry and later in a water purification unit. With a few friends, he continued his studies privately, meeting secretly to read poetry and perform plays. By 1942 he became a student in the underground seminary in Kraków run by Archbishop Adam Stefan Sapieha. At one point, in 1944, he barely escaped a Gestapo roundup and he went into hiding in the archbishop's residence. And, when Kraków was liberated by the Russians in January 1945, he narrowly escaped arrest a second time.

Before the borders were sealed in 1946 the promising student was sent to Rome for further training. That same year Sapieha was named a cardinal, but until his death in 1951 he refused to wear his cardinal's robes: "I shall not wear them so long as my country is suffering," he explained.

After his return from Rome in 1948, Father Wojtyła served small churches in or near Kraków, carefully avoiding provocative political activities, though he was popular with youth and continued his interest in literature and drama. It is estimated that during the reign of Stalin at least two thousand bishops, priests and Catholic lay persons were imprisoned. The primate, Stefan Cardinal Wyszyński, was for three years confined to a monastery in Eastern Poland. By 1958, after Stalin's death, there was talk of "the Polish spring" and the yoke on the church was somewhat lighter. That was the year that Father Wojtyła was named a bishop. During the decade that followed, there was a quiet and for the most part spiritual struggle between the church and the state for the allegiance of the people, the great majority of whom were at least nominal Catholics. The official doctrine taught in the schools and evident in the press was that Poland had become a model of socialism. The church, however, continued to teach that for nine hundred years Poland had been a fortress of Christian liberty.

One of the battlegrounds of the spiritual struggle was the town of Nowa Huta, east of Kraków, the first planned city that was designed to be the birthplace of the New Socialist Man. There the Lenin plant produced two million tons of steel annually. Every day was a work day, and in the eyes of the socialist leaders there was no room for a church. The New Man had no need for religion. But Sunday after Sunday, thousands of faithful men and women gathered for devotions out in the open. When the people erected a cross, the authorities replied by allocating the area to a school. When the officials tried to remove the Christian symbol, the people replied with violent resistance. Police cars were overturned. Hundreds were arrested. During the next ten years, however, the people built a church with their own hands, bringing more than two million stones from the mountain streams. At the dedication of the church, Wojtyła — now an archbishop — spoke of human rights: religious freedom and the right to work. A passage suppressed by the official censor also described the right to a fair wage. A popular demand for that right later became the spring-

board for the rise of the Solidarity trade union. Not long
after the dedication of the Nowa Huta church, the archbishop was called to Rome to receive the red hat of a
cardinal.

During this period, the church was virtually the only
institution in the Polish society that was able to maintain its ties abroad. The Roman Catholic Church generally
was able to keep its lines to the Vatican open. Although
these contacts were often restricted, the church had long
since established the fact that it was supranational. That
fact, as well as frequent initiatives from Rome, frequently
presented troubling problems for the Communist leaders.
But because of the devotion and loyalty of such a high
percentage of the population, the government was forced
to accept it. In Poland, at least, religion was the essential
bread of the people and not, as Marx had once declared,
an opiate.

Four of the minority churches that are related to the
Polish Ecumenical Council are members of the World
Council of Churches. Two of them (the Evangelical
Church of the Augsburg Confession and the Polish Cath-
olic Church in Poland) were founding members of the
World Council; the Polish Orthodox Church joined the
WCC in 1961 and the Old Catholic Mariavite Church
became part of the council in 1969. The election of
Bishop Andrzej Wantula of the Evangelical Church of the
Augsburg Confession as vice president of the Lutheran
World Federation was a great encouragement to Polish
Lutherans. Significantly, the Polish Catholic Church in Poland originated in North America and maintains very close
ties to the U.S. Polish National Catholic Church. The
international role of these churches was not as pronounced
as that of the Roman Catholic Church, but Protestant
and Orthodox Christians also valued their contacts abroad,
partly in response to the overt oppression and partly
because they were in such a minority at home.

Hungary: Theological Dialogue and Personal Friendships

Geography and history enabled the Christians of Hungary to maintain strong connections with Roman Catholics and Protestants in the West. Their proud nation, which enjoys greater ethnic homogeneity than most of its neighbors, has long looked westward toward Austria. Catholicism is strong without being as dominant as it is in Poland. At the same time that the American colonies were forging a union of states, Joseph II issued his famous Edict of Tolerance. A decade later, in 1791, the constitutional rights of Protestants were restored. Though diverse, the Protestant churches have a long tradition of ecumenism, which since World War II has been expressed internationally as well as domestically. They lay claim, in fact, to the earliest pulpit and table fellowship expressed anywhere in the world, dating to the Nagygerezsd Agreement in 1833.

The churches of Hungary also have related to their confessional partners in other lands. The Reformed Church in Hungary has especially strong theological ties to Reformed churches in the Netherlands, Scotland and the United States. Its seminaries have an international reputation. The Reformed Church was a founding member of the World Council of Churches and of the Conference of European Churches and played a very strong role in the Christian Peace Conference (CPC). The latter organization, whose energy derived from the Central and Eastern European churches that were seeking ways to express their faith within repressive socialist societies, provided one more significant link to Christians in the West.

Within the CPC, Western Christians frequently debated the views of men like Professor Josef Hromádka of Czechoslovakia, Metropolitan Nikodim of the Russian Orthodox Church, and later Bishop Károly Tóth of Hungary. But these deep political differences were not allowed to be the cause for a break in the Christian community. To the contrary, Western church leaders accepted criticism at home in order to strengthen the bonds of fellowship and to improve their understanding of the circumstances in which their Hungarian friends were living. Bishop Tóth and several others participated frequently in these dialogues, relishing the continued contact with personal friends from the West and contributing significantly to the theological contacts that, though sometimes limited, were never ruptured.

Because these lines of communication were open, and because Western church leaders frequently visited Hungary, theological dialogue often led to personal friendships. And these personal friendships, based as they were in a shared faith, enabled a candid exchange of information and opinion across barriers. Western diplomats sometimes grudgingly admitted that Christian leaders had more reliable information than most embassy officials, in large part because the church leaders had established a personal credibility.

One example of how these ecumenical contacts were utilized by Western Christians was the widely publicized "peace conference" on "Saving the Sacred Gift of Life from Nuclear Catastrophe," sponsored in May 1982 by the Russian Orthodox Church. During that conference of Buddhists, Christians, Hindus, Jews, Muslims, Shintoists, Sikhs and Zoroastrians from ninety nations, representatives of U.S. and Canadian churches were concerned that the final communiqué, as it was being developed, seemed uncritically to echo Soviet foreign policy, as frequently was the case in Central and Eastern Europe and the USSR. Western perspectives were added during the debate, but the draft communiqué was not altered until three American Christians explained the lack of balance to their Hungarian friend Károly Tóth. William P. Thompson of the Presbyterian Church (U.S.A.), Arie R. Brouwer of the Reformed Church in America and Avery D. Post of the United Church of Christ huddled with Bishop Tóth and several others with whom they had long ecumenical ties. The three Americans had worked with the Hungarian bishop on numerous occasions, including meetings and working groups of the World Alliance of Reformed Churches. Post also utilized his contacts with East German church leaders developed through the UCC-EKU *Kirchen-gemeinschaft*, and with Central and Eastern Europeans whom he knew personally through an informal East-West church dialogue. Post was at that time the co-chairperson of the dialogue, known as Kárlovy Vary for the Czech city where its first meeting was held. Such personal friendships, developed across ideological boundaries, became the platform for persuasive conversations. The final document, the closing statements and a news conference as the meeting ended all reflected a balanced concern for peace initiatives and human rights efforts.

CHAPTER TWO

Church and State

Standing with the People

There was a poignant irony during 1989, the year of the Velvet Revolution in Czechoslovakia, when groups in several nations of Europe and the United States celebrated the centennial of the birth of Josef L. Hromádka, the controversial Czech theologian.

As Professor Charles C. West of Princeton Seminary pointed out to an organization called Christians Associated for Relations with Eastern Europe, Hromádka was a Christian "leader in whom the East and the West combined." Deeply influenced by his training and travels in the West, he was politically a socialist and a Czech nationalist. He played an important role in the World Council of Churches and was founder of the Christian Peace Conference, a deliberate effort to enable substantive conversations among Christians across the ideological barriers that followed World War II. Hromádka was, in the words of Professor West, "influential in establishing the spirit of the 'Prague Spring' in 1968" through his friendship with Marxist leaders including Alexander Dubček. He worked hard to provide socialism with a human face. He died in 1969, bitterly disappointed, a year after the Soviet invasion of Czechoslovakia crushed the liberal reforms to which he had given his energies.

One of Hromádka's former students, Milan Opočensky, is today the general secretary of the World Alliance of Reformed Churches. He speaks of the ways in which for two decades his mentor had tried to help the churches in Czechoslovakia and throughout the world "come to terms with an ideology which seems totally hostile to the church, religion and Christianity." Hromádka did so as a theologian who tried to understand not only the theory of Marxism but who also sought to learn and describe its appeal to persons who yearned for an economic balance that seemed absent in most capitalist nations. The Czech theologian also helped thousands of persons understand the dangers of both secularism and Christian triumphalism, which he demonstrated were present in both East and West. The church, Hromádka insisted, could not speak a prophetic word to Marxists without acknowledging that too often it had failed to strive for human dignity. He particularly pointed to the Holocaust, in which millions of Jews lost their lives, and to the inability of the Christian churches to mobilize themselves to act in response to that inhumanity.

Hromádka and other Christians with whom he worked closely believed that the church "is not at home under any political regime, nor under any social and economic order." They saw the church as a servant of the world, sharing the servanthood of Christ, to all who are in need. They also called on the church, through such agencies as the World Council of Churches and the Christian Peace Conference, to envision a future in which justice, freedom and peace could be universally enjoyed. As the Hungarian bishop Károly Tóth pointed out at a centennial symposium in Prague, Hromádka's view of ecumenism included appreciation for the spiritual values of non-Christian religions and especially for their contributions to human dignity. According to Opočensky, Hromádka should be considered the founder of the so-called Christian-Marxist dialogue. Certainly he risked misunderstanding and unpopularity to develop channels of communication between East and West.

Hromádka liked to speak of "looking history in the face." History, as it turned out, honored the centennial of his birth by coming full cycle since 1968. During the decades since the end of World War II, the churches learned from Hromádka and others the necessity of standing for justice, seeking a fuller understanding of the nature of human dignity, and entering into conversations with ideological opponents to create more humane societies.

Such understandings could have developed only in Central and Eastern Europe, although they greatly influenced individuals and churches in North America and Western Europe. Their legacy is especially to be found in the commitment of the churches to look beyond institutional welfare and to find ways to help persons in need regardless of their religious affiliations. That commitment was demonstrated in many Eastern countries where church leaders steadfastly remained to serve their people when they might have defected rather easily to the West. Instead they encouraged their neighbors not to leave, believing that the future of their countries requires the best that citizens can offer. In many situations, these forthright pastors and church leaders risked personal difficulties in order to express to government leaders the people's needs for greater freedoms and improved conditions.

The impulse for this servanthood was described by Steven and Gratia Johns-Boehme in a report published by the Europe/USSR office of the National Council of Churches of Christ in the U.S.A.: "The voice of the church in the German Democratic Republic will be the living out of a statement made at [its] synod in September 1989: 'In following Jesus Christ, life is not fulfilled in that which I have for myself, but in that which I am for others.' [The voice of the church] will be the continued application of

Dietrich Bonhoeffer's recognition that 'the reason for the existence of the church is found only in its being there for others.'" In an article in *Christianity and Crisis* magazine, Barbara Green described the significance of Bonhoeffer's quotation for Christians in the former German Democratic Republic: "It attempts to call the church away from protecting its own interests or developing its own privileges and to pastoral responsibility for others, including non-Christians." Like the Johns-Boehmes, Green worked with Christians in GDR, in her case from 1977 to 1981.

Conversations with Government Leaders

Conversations between religious leaders and government officials over the four decades following the end of World War II were sometimes tense, always problematic, but nonetheless very significant.

In the German Democratic Republic, the churches played an intermediary role between the state and the people and as a result established high credibility with both. From the beginning of the immediate post–World War II period, the churches were able to maintain an independent position, rather than the governmental one. There is a dramatic story of how Bishop Moritz Mitzenheim of Thuringia established his ecclesiastical authority with the Soviet occupation forces. Mitzenheim had staunchly resisted Hitler when other Christians in Thuringia had not. As the Russian army moved into Eisenach he decided to try to develop good working relationships. He invited the Russian commandant to his palace located atop a hill facing the historic Wartburg Castle across the valley on another hilltop. The bishop led the Russian general to the cellar and showed him a huge cross. "Hitler's fascists took this cross from the tower of the castle," he said. "Your soldiers will put it back." And they did. His successors, knowing the story, sought to remain as firm in the faith and as self-confident personally as Bishop Mitzenheim had been.

The Evangelical Church in Germany, the EKD, is a federation of Lutheran, Reformed and United churches. From the end of the war until 1969, the EKD functioned as a united body although Germany had been divided into two states. Finally, in 1969, under great pressure from officials of the German Democratic Republic, East Germans separated themselves from the West. Eventually when a separate church federation was organized the Federation of Evangelical Churches in the GDR insisted that its purpose was functional and that the spiritual ties with the West German church could not be broken. From the beginning, the federation called on the government of the GDR to provide greater openness and through the federation the churches worked for change within the society.

East German theologians honestly struggled to understand socialist values as proclaimed by Marxists. In the mid-1960s, they initiated efforts for a Christian-Marxist dialogue. In 1982 the Güstrow Colloquium was established as the setting for an annual convocation of Christian theologians, Marxists philosophers and scientists. Similar dialogues in other Central and Eastern European countries, as well as in the West, helped demonstrate to Communist officials that church leaders were seeking to operate in the best interests of the people. The International Conference of Systematic Theologians of Socialist Countries provided the forum for comparable discussions involving not only East Germans but Czechs and Hungarians as well.

The leaders of the church in the GDR early agreed to offer the Communist authorities a kind of "conditional allegiance." They would reject policies of the government only when conscience required it. Two theologians, Johannes Hempel and Günter Jakob, outlined the basis for what they called a theology of "critical solidarity." The church would cooperate with all that was defensible; it would openly critique all that was indefensible. They spoke of a "church not alongside of, not against, but within socialism." That formula became the principle by which Albrecht Schönherr, a student of Dietrich Bonhoeffer during the Nazi period and under the Communists the first president of the East German Church Federation, worked with the authorities. Bishop Schönherr helped shape the church's witness in East Germany's socialist society by urging the churches to work from the faith that "if God's free grace is the ultimate reality in the world, nothing can separate us from the love of God."

Eventually the government formally agreed to deal with the church as the only major social force that it did not directly control. In 1971, when the federation declared its willingness to work as a "church within socialism," the state eased its overt repression. Two years later, the federation defined the church within socialism as "the church which helps the individual Christian and the individual congregation to find their way within both the freedom and the discipline of the faith, and to pursue what is best for all society."

In March 1978, at a meeting between church and state representatives, the Honecker government officially recognized the autonomy of the church. The government accepted as a rule of thumb a statement proposed by the churches that "the relationship between the state and the church is only as good as individual Christian citizens experience it in their local situations." That statement provided a base line for dealing with individual cases of discrimination. Honecker also gave pastors and designated lay persons the right to visit prisons and provided limited access to radio and television broadcasting. In an arrangement that was never publicly acknowledged, the East German church was permitted to receive significant financial subsidies from its West German counterpart. This, of course, not only helped the churches in the GDR but also provided an infusion of hard currency into the country's foundering economy. It is estimated that during the last forty years, the Evangelical Church in (West) Germany gave nearly two billion deutsche mark to the churches in East Germany. This would be the equivalent of $1,183,400,000 at present exchange rates.

Honecker apparently recognized that his struggling regime needed the stability that the churches could provide. He dealt with the church leaders on their concerns because he needed their help in fighting the rampant problem of alcoholism. The courageous pastors, however, were always wary of the government. Occasionally the police checked the identification of persons entering the churches. Plainclothes officers sometimes infiltrated church meetings to discover the church strategies and even to disrupt plans by raising intimidating questions. Nevertheless, the church spoke critically and persistently on such global and local concerns as nuclear disarmament and human rights.

The same year that it had acknowledged the autonomy of the churches, the government began paramilitary training in the public high schools. The church criticized the effort and launched its own peace education programs. Nonviolence was taught as a political strategy and youth were introduced to the thought of Martin Luther King, Jr. In 1983, when the North Atlantic Treaty Organization decided to deploy cruise and Pershing II missiles in Western Europe, the churches in the GDR called for discussions on peace. These programs provided the commitment to nonviolence and the infrastructure that kept the demonstrations of 1989 peaceful.

Because it operated with relatively minimal interference in its internal affairs and because the pastors increasingly were concerned about the impact of heavy industry on the region's delicate ecology and about the desires of young workers to emigrate, the East German church provided the soil in which the ideas of a new society began to germinate. The church opened its doors to young people — many of whom were secular persons without personal ties to religion — and to men and women who were discontented with their lot. For nearly a decade these persons were welcomed to the weekly prayers for peace with justice. Those services, especially in Berlin and Leipzig, provided the seedbed for radical social change.

The Protestant churches thus became places where various groups could meet, including environmentalists, feminists, gay persons and a number of dissident organizations. Because the churches were based on a different ideology from other social institutions in the Marxist state, groups meeting in churches were able to express a variety of concerns. For the most part, this role of the churches was accepted as legitimate by most believers, although at first there was some modest controversy over the way the church had become a patron of and shelter for the alternative youth subculture. But as the issues developed, the churches urged state officials to be more tolerant of the newly vocal groups in the society. On occasion, church leaders carried messages back to the dissident groups, thereby insulating them from direct confrontation and possible disciplinary action. The political officials were obviously pleased when Protestant church leaders all during the period discouraged people from fleeing and later from emigrating to the West. For their part, the church officials expressed the conviction that those who leave will forfeit their ability and right to contribute to the renewal of the nation. It was therefore significant that, in 1989, when travel rights were broadened the government informed the church before any public announcement was made.

During these years the much smaller Roman Catholic Church in the GDR took a very different approach. Cardinal Bengsch consistently felt that Roman Catholics should abstain from all public involvement. According to some, this was a period of "hibernation" in which without either approving or criticizing government policy the church simply waited for better times. Like the Protestant bodies, it relied on support from the West. By the time the revolution was underway in East Germany, Pope John Paul II urged Catholics in Berlin to "do everything you can — even as a small flock — to join with all people of good will, especially with Protestant Christians, in order to renew the face of the earth in your land through the power of the Spirit of God."

CHAPTER THREE

Church for the People

Advocates for Human Rights

During the years of oppression, church leaders and Christian lay persons in nearly all the Central and East European nations were courageous advocates for human rights.

Among those in Hungary who suffered for their criticism of the state's treatment of the Hungarian people was Lutheran Bishop Lajos Ordass. He was removed from office in 1950 for speaking out against the Communist officials. Eventually he was released, but when he refused to change his views he was removed again in 1958 and spent a total of twenty years under house arrest. Although Bishop Ordass died in 1978, his courage and example are still frequently mentioned. The Evangelical Lutheran Church in Hungary, which had conducted occasional services at his grave, in December 1989 requested that all accusations against the late bishop be withdrawn. When changes came to Hungary, the new minister of justice cleared the Ordass name on May 1, 1990, and admitted that the removal of the bishop from office was unfounded. On behalf of the new government in Hungary, the Minister of Justice asked forgiveness from the church and from the bishop's widow.

Certainly the attention that the churches and other groups gave to the issue of human rights was a significant factor that helped build pressure for change in Central and Eastern Europe. Many church workers credit the emphasis on the Helsinki accords process and the way in which individuals and organizations watched intently for infractions of human rights agreements and reported publicly on such violations, with the initiation of political action. The thirty-five nations that participated in the Conference on Security and Cooperation in Europe and that signed the Helsinki Final Act in 1975 agreed to work toward the promotion of disarmament, economic cooperation and increased human contacts and human rights. They also agreed to a monitoring process in which year after year they came together to hear reports on progress and on areas in which additional work was needed. The process that was established encouraged church groups and other organizations to join in what became known as Helsinki Watch committees. As it turned out, in Central and Eastern Europe the churches were virtually the only indigenous associations that had the international contacts to make their efforts significant and credible.

From 1980 to 1985 Christa Lewek chaired the international Churches' Human Rights Program for the Implementation of the Helsinki Final Act. The work, which often described the plight of East Germans, was directed from Lewek's office as secretary for church and society of the Federation of Evangelical Churches in the GDR. The Human Rights Program was co-sponsored by the U.S. National Council of Churches, the Canadian Council of Churches and the Conference of European Churches. Not infrequently the federation communicated its concerns about the conditions in the GDR to government officials whose response usually was polite but empty.

In 1980 the federation developed a program dedicated to a witness through word and service to the cause of peace. The federation adopted a theological statement that provided a focus for its work:

- Forgiveness, which makes possible one's own action and one's own first steps, even when they involve risk.

- The privilege of encouraging others, without concern for one's self, to exhibit freedom from prejudice, openness and temperance in negotiations and discussions.

- The admonition given in God's Word to see ourselves, the church and our own country critically.

- The prayer that within and beyond our activity the final decision be left to God.

From this theological statement and the program it represented, a national event called Ten Days for Peace, or *Friedensdekade*, was organized, largely in response to the state's paramilitary program for high school youth. During November each year since 1980 local churches all across the GDR planned workshops and celebrations and arranged for peace prayers. Correspondence with Christians in other nations was encouraged. The program particularly appealed to youth, and the church was seen as offering the place where thoughtful discussions could take place. Methodist Bishop Rüdiger Minor cites a 1988 survey showing that 40 percent of Methodist youth had become conscientious objectors to both military training and military service. The church found itself in the position of having to interpret the theological views of its youth to the government.

Beginning in 1983 the Nikolaikirche and many other churches in other cities began holding Monday evening prayer services in response to the deployment of cruise and Pershing missiles. By 1989 these had become well-established events to which many came, looking for a place in which to speak of their convictions. People came whether or not they were related to the Christian faith.

The pastors at the St. Nicholas Church, and other congregations that later adopted what became known as the
Leipzig model, spoke frequently of the grace of God that
is not dependent on an individual's religious orientation.

The commitment to human rights among East German church leaders derives from several sources. Among
them there are numerous men and women who honor the
memory of Dietrich Bonhoeffer, a theologian who helped
to organize the so-called Confessing Church and who ran
a clandestine seminary in opposition to Hitler. A few,
in fact, had been students of Bonhoeffer, who was executed on Hitler's orders just before the end of World
War II. Many of the contemporary German Christian leaders recognize that the organized church failed to speak out
unequivocally against the Nazis.

During the first half of the Communist period in
Czechoslovakia, the theologian Josef Hromádka worked to
help provide "socialism with a human face." After the
Prague Spring was ended by the military intervention of
Soviet troops in 1968, a number of Protestant and Roman
Catholic clergy and laity placed their hopes in the human
rights accords signed in Helsinki. On January 1, 1977,
a group of church persons, artists, actors and academics
signed a declaration that came to be known as Charter 77.

Those who agreed to work for broadening human and
civil rights announced that they were a "free, informal,
open community of people of different convictions, different faiths, and different professions." They emphasized
that they were not an organization and that their charter did not "form the basis of any opposition political
activity." They knew, of course, that it would be illegal
to form any kind of independent organization, much less
an oppositional political group. The regime gave them little opportunity to organize; they were watched and their
friends were watched; their phones were tapped; they were
intimidated; some were imprisoned; all were subject to be
assigned to menial tasks.

Some Protestants and Roman Catholics were "Chartists" — but they were relatively few. Such participation was discouraged by the churches. From the early part of the Communist period, Roman Catholic monastic orders were closed. Two-thirds of the monks were shipped to forced labor camps. Enough priests, theologians and bishops were imprisoned to make all others wary. Bishoprics went unfilled after the Vatican's appointee to Hradec Králové was put to work as a milkman. One group of priests, an organization known as Pacem in Terris, clearly was loyal to the state and not to Rome. Not infrequently Protestant clergy were coerced by the state, which paid their salaries, approved their appointments and made lay participation in congregations difficult and often unpleasant. Although there were one thousand signatories in 1977, the remaining "Chartists" were relatively few. Many of the original thousand had been imprisoned. Others had emigrated. Some had publicly resigned. But, thanks in part to Václav Benda, a Catholic lay person, Charter 77 survived. After his four years in prison, he took up responsibility for speaking out for the Chartists. One task they had agreed upon was to keep alive the memory of such persons as Tomáš Garrigue Masaryk, the pre-war president of the Czech Republic. They did so in many ways, including the publication of underground journals and papers, the secretly distributed *samizdat*.

Václav Havel, a popular author who also had been imprisoned for his activities, continued to write plays and essays because, for him, the question was how deeply the truth embedded in the Charter of 1977 was penetrating the society. Although he makes no claim to be a practicing Christian, he was clearly regarded as a moral leader whose writings communicated spiritual insights. His *Letters to Olga*, written while he was in prison, are both an argument against the totalitarian state and a call to spiritual renewal. Havel speaks of reading the Bible, of his "affinity for Christian sentiment," but explains that he "accepts the Gospel of Jesus as a challenge to go my own way."

Twenty years after the Prague Spring abruptly ended, a modest but courageous Roman Catholic peasant from a Moravian village proved that an individual can help a nation speak for human rights. Augustin Navrátil works in a railway station. Beginning in 1976 he began writing petitions. The first, which he drafted with a neighbor, dealt with local issues and contained seventeen points. He collected seven hundred signatures — and an extended visit to a psychiatric hospital. The next time, in 1984, he first sent his twenty-point petition to all the government ministries that he could think of. A covering letter asked, "Is it legal to circulate this?" There were no replies, but there was a second trip to the psychiatric ward of the prison hospital. A judge declared that he was a danger to a society and he was detained a year. On release, he was thoroughly beaten up by what were officially termed "unknown assailants."

By 1987 he had obtained notarized permission to operate a home duplicator, a simple silk screen machine. "The citizen does not require a permit . . . to employ duplicating equipment for his own use," the permission letter said. With the duplicator he produced open letters, petitions, copies of official responses, and an annotated list of the vacant Roman Catholic dioceses. His masterpiece was a petition in which he called for freedom for the church. In the context of the repression of religious organizations in Czechoslovakia, it was a significant appeal for basic human rights.

Navrátil's thirty-one demands called not only for freedom for church publications but for separation of church and state and for the right of the church to appoint bishops without interference. The archbishop of Prague, František Cardinal Tomášek, wrote an open letter urging the faithful to support the petition. "I recall most emphatically that cowardice and fear are unworthy of a true

Christian," wrote the aging Cardinal Tomášek, who himself was born in Moravia. The railroad worker reprinted the cardinal's letter on his little machine and handed it out with copies of the petition.

Incredibly, in a nation with harsh penalties for less subversive activities, nearly half a million Czechs, some who were not even Roman Catholics, signed Navrátil's petition in 1988. Even in the bleak Moravian mid-winter, there was a touch of spring in the air. One human being had effectively witnessed for the rights of many others.

Ministries to Those in Need

In the German Democratic Republic, the churches' diaconal ministries were continued during a time when socialist governments in other countries insisted that social services were the sole responsibility of the state. It was in the GDR that some of these ministries have been pioneered on the basis of carefully articulated theological principles. More than in most other nations, the churches in the GDR saw these services as essential expressions of the faith. Even persons who did not themselves participate in congregations expected the churches to provide health care and other services.

Church-sponsored hospitals, homes for the elderly, therapy and learning centers for the physically and mentally handicapped and other facilities were recognized by state health care and social welfare programs in the German Democratic Republic. The basic operating costs, including salaries, were covered by the state while clergy persons and deacons serving in administrative positions were paid by the church.

Protestants and Roman Catholics operated 76 hospitals. Protestants ran an additional 100 residential facilities, 23 day care centers for mentally handicapped persons, 149 convalescent centers and 218 retirement homes. Diaconal

ministries to handicapped persons were of special significance. The memory of Nazi crimes against the physically
and mentally impaired remains vivid, and the churches
won the trust of communities as they provided not only
well-equipped day care centers but also professionally
directed therapy and support groups for parents. In addition, ministries to troubled youth, to persons addicted to
alcohol and other drugs and to persons released from prisons were developed in 141 urban missions without any
government support.

Such programs, many of which had roots going back
to pre-World War II days, played an important role in developing and maintaining both credibility with the people
and an ongoing dialogue with the government. These diaconal ministries were seen as evidence that the church
exists for service.

Part II

Leadership for Liberation

Since last December, people with hammers and chisels go at the Berlin Wall, to break a piece out of the concrete panels. They are now called "wall-peckers." I think Christians should become such wall-peckers, to overcome divisiveness with patience and hope, in peace and with persistence, in love and protest.

— The Rev. Wolfgang Steckel of Dessau, German Democratic Republic, in a sermon prepared for use on February 4, 1990, in the five partnership churches located in Dessau; Hartford, Connecticut; Ostrava, Czechoslovakia; Purley, England; and Speyer, Federal Republic of Germany

55

CHAPTER FOUR

Poland: The Church Stands with Labor

The dramatic events that took place in the fall of 1989 not only have changed the lives of millions of persons in Central and Eastern Europe but also have impacted the futures of people around the world. Those momentous events began as small decisions, halting — even uncertain — steps. They have demonstrated, among other things, that even in authoritarian societies, individuals of goodwill and courage can make a difference.

What happened in Central and Eastern Europe is the story of peoples; it is also the story of a relatively few persons whose commitment to the biblical faith, to peace and to human dignity empowered risk-taking action. Whether they articulated it or not, they agreed with the East German pastor Wolfgang Steckel, who believes that "Christians are challengers who keep demonstrating in front of dividing walls, who attack these walls with hammers and chisels until stones and concrete blocks loosen, so that the face of the person behind the wall becomes visible."

No one who was involved would have predicted that

the simple acts that were taken would have been so world-changing. One act encouraged another and then another and another. When three Hungarian church leaders responded to the urgent desires of East German tourists, soldiers cut a stretch of barbed wire fence. It was the first crevice that became an avalanche. Within weeks, the Wall where so many had died came tumbling down. Within months, Germany was resurrected.

The reports that follow describe how, in country after country, men and women — related in one way or another to the church — helped eliminate the walls that divide.

Ask any Pole when the change began. The answer, from government official, Roman Catholic nun, Protestant youth or Solidarity ship builder, always will be the same.

Two elections, they'll say. Both beyond their borders. One was in March 1985 when Mikhail Gorbachev — the man who taught the world the meaning of a pair of Russian words, *glasnost* and *perestroika* — was selected as general secretary of the Communist Party in the USSR. Gorbachev made the change possible, permitted it to happen. Some even believe that the Soviet leader encouraged the changes in Central and Eastern Europe because he recognized that change also must take place in the Soviet Union. On December 8, 1988, Gorbachev announced the unilateral withdrawal of part of the Soviet military forces in the Warsaw Pact countries and affirmed that there can be "different roads to socialism." On July 7, 1989, he went further: "How the Polish and Hungarian people decide to structure their society and their lives will be their affair. . . . Any attempts to restrict the sovereignty of states — friends, allies or any others — are inadmissible."

The other election was in 1978 when the Sacred College of Cardinals, meeting for the second time in two months, stunned the world by picking Karol Wojtyła as pope. With well-chosen words and carefully orchestrated actions the Holy Father inspired the people of Poland and authorized their actions. Without personally directing the drama in his homeland, in effect he wrote the script.

Eventually historians will take the measure of these two men and deal with their weaknesses and blind spots as well as their charisma and their courage. But, in any case, history will never be the same. In an era in which thousands played major roles on the world's stage, these men were central.

Perhaps no one was more surprised at the outcome of the conclave in Rome than the Polish Communist Party chief, Edward Gierek. The papers on October 16, 1978, screamed the headline with a mixture of Latin and Polish: *Habemus Papam!* the traditional announcement, "We have a pope!" and the name, Jan Pawel II. Gierek rose to the occasion and sent a telegram of congratulations. The president of Poland, Henryk Jablonski, led two thousand Poles to the pope's inauguration in Rome. But Gierek soon made it clear that the Communist politicians did not want the immensely popular advocate of the faith to return to Poland for a victory celebration.

The pope, of course, wanted to visit his homeland, especially to return to Kraków, which he had left expecting a relatively short conclave. After a reasonable time — nearly a year — he let it be known that he wanted to visit Poland on the nine hundredth anniversary of the death of St. Stanislaus. Ever since he was assassinated by King Boleslaw the Bold for opposing royal policies, Stanislaus has been the national symbol of church resistance to oppression. The government could not accept such overt provocation. May is inconvenient, they replied to John Paul II in a diplomatic "Nothing doing." But come in June, if you must. We won't do anything to block the visit and we won't do anything to facilitate it either.

The pope would not be outdone. He simply announced that, by papal decree, the celebration honoring the Polish saint would be extended until after his visit. The quiet anger of the officials was evident only to the church officials who had to do all the planning, manage all the protocol, arrange all the logistics. The eight-day visit was spectacular, from the now traditional kissing of the ground as he stepped from the plane to a mid-day mass for hundreds of thousands at the Monastery of Jasna Gora, where the black Madonna icon hangs in the Shrine to Our Lady of Czestochowa. As they planned and executed the papal visit, the officials and laity of the Polish church learned that they could, with impunity, face down the government. And they cultivated a network of workers that bloomed again two years later as Solidarity.

All during the visit the pope chose his words skillfully. He spoke of the rights of workers and the value of labor. The latter, he said, should be understood as a service to humanity rather than as a dominating force. The workers cheered. In Warsaw the crowd interrupted his sermon when he asserted, "Christ is at the center. Christ cannot be kept out of history in any part of the globe. The exclusion of Christ from the history of humanity is an act against humanity." It was a powerful thing to say in a city where the government insisted that atheism be taught in the schools. At first, there was scattered applause. Then songs of faith. And finally chants: "We want God! We want God!"

At one point, when the crowd greeted him with a traditional song, *Sto-Lat*, wishing him a hundred years of life, the pope turned to his mentor, Cardinal Wyszyński. During the Stalinist period, when the church suffered greatly, Wyszyński had become the symbol of the defiant resistance of the church. There was another verse of *Sto-Lat* for the seventy-eight-year-old primate.

The eight days of the pope's visit were filled with songs, cheers and sermons — and with an eloquent silence. On the same day that he returned to the church in Wadowice, where he had been baptized, John Paul II also went to Auschwitz and Birkenau, where four million Jews and Poles were killed by the Nazis. He knelt silently in the cell where Maximilian Kolbe, a Franciscan priest, offered his own life in place of a man marked for extermination. Then the pope spoke of the tragedy of war. "A fifth of this nation lost their lives during World War II. Yet another stage in the centuries-old fight of this nation, my nation, for its fundamental rights among the peoples of Europe. Yet another loud cry for the right to a place of its own on the map of Europe...."

After those June days in 1979, the pope in Rome found many ways to speak to the spirit of the Polish people. His message of words and deeds inspired not only the Roman Catholic majority but Protestants as well. It is said that the name of the labor movement, *Solidarnosc*, was suggested by the pope's appeal in the encyclical *Redemptor hominis*, "The Redeemer of humanity," for people to act together to insure the dignity of each human being as a child of God.

Today in the "new Poland," many Protestants, like the director of the Polish Bible Society, Barbara Engholc-Narzynska and her husband, Lutheran Bishop Janusz Narzynski, are concerned that political pluralism has not yet been translated into confessional pluralism. But they watched with appreciation as John Paul II found ways to encourage the Polish people from a distance.

Because so much of Polish tradition and history is linked to Catholic piety, the efforts of Communist leaders to create new values and new models were fruitless. More than people in any other Central or Eastern European nation, Poles retained religious ceremonies and symbols. In 1981, workers in the Lenin shipyard in Gdansk erected towering steel crosses in memory of their colleagues who had been killed in a 1970 confrontation with Communist authorities. And because of its overwhelming size, the Roman Church furnished most of the leadership of the Solidarity movement. The courageous and determined leader Lech Wałęsa openly displayed his piety. Photographs of Wałęsa with the pope helped inspire support and provided a measure of protection for the trade union in its early days.

The Catholic people of Poland often looked to their church for encouragement and guidance. It was natural, therefore, that priests like Father Józef Tischner provided the philosophy of the emerging movement. In his foreword to Tischner's 1984 book, *The Spirit of Solidarity*, Zbigniew Brzezinski explained that the Solidarity movement is motivated by simple religious faith and is committed to peaceful action. Brzezinski, who was President Jimmy Carter's national security adviser, introduced Father Tischner as the outstanding church teacher in linking theology to the quest for social justice, "a truly major figure."

Tischner, who himself has insisted that "not everyone in Poland should be Catholic," explains that "in this pope there is something that everyone can accept." The priest once wrote, "Whatever we might say about the popes, one thing is certain; the popes know what history is. They know what truly lasts in history and what passes away like the grass in the autumn. The popes have a duty to remind us of what is indestructible, so that people and nations might tie their fates with what lasts."

From the very beginning of Solidarity, Father Tischner helped shape its direction. He had met with the striking workers in August 1980 at the same Gdansk shipyard where a decade earlier an undisclosed number of workers were shot to death by Communist authorities for a similar demonstration. He met them on their lunch breaks, where they knelt for confession and then received Holy Communion. The philosopher in him asked, "What does it mean to be in solidarity?" He answered his own question by quoting Galatians 6:2: "Carry one another's burdens and in this way fulfill God's law." Solidarity means "to carry the burden of another person. . . . We are bound to each other. . . . The landscape binds us, flesh and blood bind us, work and speech bind us."

The gutsy young priest, who taught at the theological faculty in Kraków, went to the citadel on Wawel Hill, not far from his Institute of Philosophy. From the eleventh to the sixteenth centuries the citadel was the capital of Poland. There, in the cathedral of Bishop Stanislaus, he cited the courage and faith of the famous Polish saint who was assassinated by the king's mercenaries while he celebrated mass. Father Tischner also reminded the workers of the words of their most recent bishop, now the pope. Less than two years earlier on the same hill John Paul II had said, "You must be strong by the strength of faith. Today you need this strength more than in any other period of history."

Tischner was the chaplain of the first Solidarity congress the next year. He insisted that the problem of the workers with the government "impinges upon human dignity — human dignity that is based on the conscience of human beings. The deepest solidarity," he said, "is solidarity of consciences." Early on he also wrote openly about democracy — in which "those governed are at the same time those who govern." He seemed to dare an official response when he wrote: "Do you wish to know what our social system truly is? Then do not ask sociologists, do not ask governors, or party secretaries; ask workers, ask farmers. Their knowledge of the system does not come to them secondhand — from reading newspapers and books... — but is inscribed on their backs by harsh daily reality."

The Solidarity strike was about bread: the price of bread and the salaries of workers. "Today, everybody — workers, farmers, intellectuals and scientists — finds a sense of dignity. The idea of dignity is in the background for all concrete hopes. Even in the call for bread, there is a call for the recognition of dignity. This is why today dignity is our democratic idea." At a communion table, Father Tischner referred to the sacred loaf. "The struggle for bread," he said, "is a struggle for human justice. How should we divide the bread so that there is enough for everyone?"

The strike made its point; the government — for a time —recognized the claim of the workers and some ten million Poles joined Solidarity. But under pressure from Moscow, Poland's Communist leaders imposed martial law in December 1981. Solidarity was outlawed and Wałęsa was confined to a hunting lodge in a remote area; it seemed that the regime could not be challenged. The times were very hard. Father Jerzy Popiełuszko, an outspoken priest who was a favorite of working people, was murdered by the secret police. Sometimes the primate, Józef Cardinal Glemp, seemed to waffle, but Rome continued to focus the world's attention on injustice in Poland.

The people remembered Solidarity, and the unique red lettering of its logo continued to appear in public places. When the pope made a second visit to Poland in 1984 the unmistakable letters were everywhere. The name of outlawed *Solidarnosc* appeared nowhere, but the familiar lettering was used in a wide variety of slogans. The papal motto, *Totus Tuus*, was prominently displayed, with the Polish flag attached to the "T." The distinctive type was used on banners reading "We greet the defender of human rights." Because they could not wear Solidarity buttons, lapel pins showing the Madonna were worn by thousands.

Chants greeted the Holy Father: "Long live the pope! Long live the pope!" and eventually the enthusiasm evoked more dangerous cheers: *So-li-dar-nosc! So-li-dar-nosc!* and *De-mo-kra-cja! Lech-Wa-łę-sa!* The pope was himself: warm, careful, correct, but forthright. The vast audience could hear and read between the lines when he spoke of love as being "greater than all the experiences and disappointments that life can prepare for us." Avoiding any direct mention of the trade union, he spoke of "fundamental solidarity between human beings." And the crowd, mostly youth, roared its approval. He concluded with a kind of benediction, especially appropriate to the place and circumstances: "Mother of Jasna Gora, you who have been given to us by Providence for the defense of the Polish nation, accept this call of Polish youth together with the Polish pope, and help us to persevere in hope."

Four years later, in May 1988, with inflation again creating severe problems for workers, another round of strikes took place. To the great dismay of the government, the workers chanted *Nie ma wolnosci bez Solidarnosci!* "There is no liberty without Solidarity!" But this time the response was different. Government officials were tired, exasperated by the economic problems. And there was a different man in the Kremlin, who was seeking to deal with his own frightening economic realities in a different way.

By August the interior minister publicly met with Wałęsa, who then used his personal credibility to end the strikes. During the next several months there were private conversations in which Solidarity sought not only an end to martial law but the legal restoration of its role in society. Finally, in January 1989, General Wojciech Jaruzelski was forced to put his own credibility on the line and press the Central Committee to accept the return of Solidarity. That opened the way for a series of Round Table talks, which began in February.

With surprising speed, an agreement was signed on April 5 that declared "the beginning of the road to parliamentary democracy." Everyone seemed surprised by the size of the opposition victory in the August elections that were only partly free. In the upper house of parliament, Solidarity won 99 of 100 seats, and thereby had the power to stall legislation. The April agreement permitted Solidarity to seek 161 seats in the ruling lower house; it won them all. Two small parties, the Peasants and the Democrats, joined a Solidarity coalition and, for the first time in history, a Communist regime was voted out of power.

The Lutheran bishop, Janusz Narzynski, was a prominent member of the top-level Round Table conversations

in 1989 that led to the elections in which the Solidarity
candidates won handily. Although the leaders of Solidarity were Roman Catholics who were empowered by the
numerical and vocal strength of their church, Wałesa and
others made it clear that the movement could not succeed
without the enthusiastic participation of other Christians
and of Jews. (The call for pluralism, however, seemed in-
tentionally to ignore those secular persons who had made
a show of their atheism.) Tadeusz Mazowiecki, the Catholic editor who befriended Solidarity and who became
prime minister after the 1989 elections, is one progressive
church member who supports the concept of a confession-
ally pluralistic state. He has encouraged the involvement
of Protestant Christians in the government of the new
Poland. Professor Tadeusz Diem of Warsaw's Polytechnic
University was named vice minister of education. Diem is
a prominent member of the Lutheran Church of the Holy
Trinity, the largest Protestant congregation in Warsaw.

CHAPTER FIVE

Hungary:
The Key Was in the Hands
of Church Leaders

Hungary had a head start.

The nation whose capital is a city of bridges that span the Danube River was perhaps the most openminded and ecumenical of the Central and Eastern European countries in matters of the faith. To be sure, under the Communists it often was difficult for congregations to keep their buildings in good repair. There were stiff limitations on church-sponsored education. But both the larger Roman Catholic Church and the somewhat smaller Reformed Church in Hungary enjoyed a measure of freedom and involvement that is rooted in historic ties with the distinctive culture.

During the thirty-seven years of Soviet domination, the Hungarian people were able to maintain both cultural and religious links with Westerners, especially with Christians. An estimated 50 percent of Hungary's Christians are Roman Catholic; 20 percent are members of the Reformed Church — which is also one of the largest Reformed bodies in Europe. Lutherans, Methodists, Baptists, Orthodox and some free churches make up the balance.

State-sponsored atheism never really took off in Hungary. Perhaps this was because the state's Office for Church Affairs was moderately lenient. Or maybe official leniency was a response to the faith and piety of the people. In any case, for years the one-chamber parliament, called the National Assembly, invited several leading church officials to sit as nonelected advisory members.

These members, like the Reformed theologian Károly Tóth, who served as president of the Ecumenical Council, were respected colleagues who had worked hard on programs that served the people. Some of Bishop Tóth's critics believe that he too quickly and too frequently supported the government's programs, especially the Soviet-oriented foreign policy. (Eventually, members of his church insisted that he distance himself from the Christian Peace Conference, which often reflected the Soviet party line on East-West issues.) Nevertheless, Bishop Tóth's presence in the parliament was significant and his behind-the-scenes influence was substantial. His national reputation was enhanced by the leadership roles he took in the World Alliance of Reformed Churches and in the World Council of Churches.

Although Tóth had been a leader in the very significant Christian-Marxist dialogues, he and his church colleagues were there to encourage the state leadership to seek greater independence from Moscow and to behave accordingly. Beginning in 1987, these changes became increasingly apparent not only in Hungary but worldwide, as Mikhail Gorbachev signaled a willingness for Hungary to experiment with greater personal freedoms and with a mixed economy. By October 1989 Dr. Tóth told Western friends, "I am glad to be associated with the men and women who are changing our society."

These changes were well underway when a delegation from the U.S. National Council of Churches visited

Hungary that month. The body of former Prime Minister Imre Nagy had been reburied with state honors. He had been executed for his role in the 1956 Revolution. The symbolic red stars were being removed from government buildings. The stores in Budapest were not only well stocked, but the displays were colorful in the Western style. Imre Pozsgay, then minister of state, spoke confidently of the experimentation with a mixed economy and said that Soviet economists not only welcomed the Hungarian model, but considered it a kind of laboratory worth watching.

Bibles and religious literature were being imported in significant quantities and a Hungarian Bible Council was preparing a new translation of the scriptures in Hungarian. Roman Catholic orders, some of which had been closed completely in the early 1950s, were now beginning to operate freely. One of Dr. Tóth's parliamentary friends, Barna Sarkadi-Nagy, who became deputy prime minister, asserted in 1988 that "the state does not want to interfere with the life of the church." In religion-conscious Hungary, this was considered a major human rights achievement.

The State Office for Church Affairs had been closed down on June 13, 1989, and laws were being prepared to guarantee freedom of conscience and religious expression. An alternative to the mandatory term of military service was being planned, an especially significant move since the government frequently had arrested members of the Bulanyist group who conscientiously adhered to nonviolence. Furthermore, the appointment of church pastors and officials no longer would require state approval. And even before it changed its name and orientation, the Communist Party categorically stated that atheism was not a prerequisite to party membership and participation.

A number of highly symbolic events demonstrated the reality of the official rhetoric. The most famous Lutheran secondary school in the country was permitted to reopen after thirty-seven years. The Budapest Evangelical Gymnasium had been closed by its Lutheran sponsors after Hungary nationalized the schools. At first the gymnasium had been granted an exception to the nationalization decree because of its world reputation (its graduates had included John von Neumann, whose mathematical theories led to the invention of the computer, physicist Eugene Wigner, explorer Sir Aurel Stein, and conductor Antal Dorati). The Lutheran minority, however, could not afford to maintain this "national treasure."

But by 1988 the old building had been made available again. After being completely refurbished the Evangelical Gymnasium was reopened under the direction of Dr. Gabor Gyapay, who years before had attended the school and later taught history there. One big change however: the reborn gymnasium enrolls girls as well as boys — an improvement, according to Dr. Gyapay.

In 1989, a historic open-country Reformed church near Tiszafured was rebuilt and rededicated. The church building had fallen into disrepair when farmers in a nearby Soviet-style collective were discouraged from attending services by being assigned Sunday tasks. Through its ministry to a neighboring institution for the handicapped, the congregation had achieved positive recognition. The rededication included a new parish educational building, another mark of changing times.

In Budapest, Methodists were offered an ideal location for a new church building, near high-rise apartments and close to a tourist and shopping center. They hope to develop the site quickly since it is considered important to the church's program of evangelism. Also in Budapest, the International Baptist Lay Academy has been built to offer biblical and theological studies to lay pastors and lay leaders throughout Central and Eastern Europe.

But certainly the most far-reaching involvement of the churches came as they sought to respond to the plight of refugees and tourists. Extreme pressures on ethnic Hungarians living in Romania had forced many to seek refuge in Hungary. The Ceausescu regime was seeking to raze several thousand villages of persons of Hungarian background living in the Transylvanian area. At the same time, large numbers of East German tourists had arrived (up to two million vacationed in Hungary each year) and many preferred not to return to their homes. With their high commitment to human rights, the churches mounted an ecumenical ministry to the Romanian and East German refugees.

And then, in a remarkable appeal, Bishop Tóth, the Roman Catholic Primate László Cardinal Paskai and Dr. László Lehel, general secretary of the Ecumenical Council, urged the government to open the border to Austria and guarantee the East Germans safe passage. The government, still led by members of the former Communist Party, agreed. Soldiers with wirecutters opened the fences. Landmines were carefully removed. The frontier was opened so that East Germans and later Czechs and Romanian refugees walked safely and easily into Austria. There they were welcomed and provided with transportation to West Germany. The first chink in the Berlin Wall had been chipped away.

When Hungary's new National Assembly opened on May 2, 1990, it was addressed by Msgr. Bela Varga, an eighty-seven-year-old Roman Catholic priest who had been forced to flee from Hungary in June 1947. He had been a leader in the Smallholders Party, which opposed the Nazis and had protected Jews, Polish refugees and French soldiers who had escaped from German prison camps. At the end of World War II, Varga was the speaker of the last free parliament, but since the 1947 Communist coup in Hungary, Varga had lived in the United States. Invited to return to Hungary in 1990 to address the first session of the new assembly, he gave thanks to "the statesman and leader of the great Russian empire as he has closed the saddest chapter in the relations of his great nation with our small one." But Varga expressed his "greatest earthly gratitude" to the Magyar [Hungarian] people "who preserved their love of freedom during more than four decades."

These changes in Hungary made it possible for the Reformed Church to undertake a number of additional social service activities that formerly had been considered the exclusive domain of the state. (As in the Soviet Union, it had been assumed that a socialist state could and should provide for all the social service needs of the people, though in Hungary the churches had maintained institutions for the aged and handicapped.) By early 1990 the churches were providing a "Mission for Saving Alcoholics," a mission for young people who lack love, understanding and support, a mission for blind and deaf-mute people, a mission for leprous people in Asia, Africa and New Guinea, a mission to gypsies and a "service for protecting marriage and family."

CHAPTER SIX

German Democratic Republic: The Church for Others

As the momentum for change across Central and Eastern Europe built steadily in 1989, the Federation of Evangelical (Protestant) Churches in the German Democratic Republic publicly advocated and privately urged the government to take steps toward a more open and progressive society. There were no surprises in its approach. For years the churches had been saying essentially the same thing.

But in May 1989 there was a growing sense of anger when published reports indicated that 98.5 percent of the voters had approved the so-called Unified List of candidates. Many East Germans knew this to be false and church poll-watchers amassed evidence of election fraud. With audacious courage, several groups of young Christians observed the ballot counting and posted their findings. Eventually the chief of the election commission, Egon Krenz, admitted that elections in the GDR were a mere "folding of paper." Feelings smoldered just below the proper and carefully polite surface.

Then the government of Erich Honecker poured adulation on the harsh, hardlining style of Nicolae Ceausescu in what many regarded as an intended slap at the policy of *perestroika*. The church press in East Germany responded with an analysis of the economic distress of the people of Romania. The deliberate response was noteworthy because only a year before Honecker's police censured or limited the distribution of church periodicals at least thirty times. That had led to a street demonstration in support of the rights of church papers, and the respected state secretary for religious affairs, Klaus Gysi, resigned.

The smoldering anger turned to burning outrage in early June 1989 when the East German *Volkskammer*, the parliament, praised the military intervention of the Chinese in Tiananmen Square. Like the Chinese, the East Germans were facing a celebration of the fortieth anniversary of their regime.

The population, increasingly distraught with the economy and with the intransigence of the leaders who had no interest in either *glasnost* or *perestroika*, was becoming restless. Their environment seemed totally polluted. Many of the medieval villages and towns were virtually ruined. Medical care was breaking down. Increasing numbers began expressing their frustrations with their feet. Many turned their back on their homeland, leaving via the embassies of the Federal Republic of Germany in Budapest, Prague and Warsaw. During early 1989, an average of two thousand persons a day left the GDR for the Federal Republic.

Beginning in March, there were demonstrations every Monday evening in Leipzig. Now these were punctuated with shouts of *Wir wollen raus!* "We want to leave!" The demonstrations followed the regular prayer services at the Nikolaikirche, services that since 1981 had been held to pray for peace and to provide voice to the voiceless and hope to the hopeless. By September 1989 this St. Nicholas Church and the St. Thomas Church, where Johann Sebastian Bach had been the music director and where he is buried, had become places for prayer where activists could find out what was happening in the movement.

All through the 1980s many churches in East Germany had provided "free rooms" or "open spaces" to a growing number of groups, places in which people could meet and feel relatively safe in the discussion of political issues. They came to those rooms in churches across the GDR to talk about many topics, from peace to the environment. They also came to develop strategies. Bishop Werner Leich, who headed the Federation of Evangelical Churches, earlier had counseled pastors and churches not to become part of opposition groups. But as the free rooms developed he said, "The church must always help in the conversations." He believes that the church must now help people find a new language, the language of freedom. Reinhardt Frank Enders of Leipzig, who in the fall of 1989 was studying at the Lutheran Seminary in Gettysburg, Pennsylvania, explained that "the church does not participate as an institution, but provides 'a Round Table' allowing different groups to talk with one another." These settings became central to the changes that took place.

One church in which the free rooms played a particularly significant role was at the Samaritan United Church in the East Berlin district known as Berlin-Friedrichshain. Sixteen years after entering the ministry, Pastor Rainer Eppelmann was an important part of the democracy movement. "You always see Eppelmann these days on television," according to Irene Runge, a sociology professor at the famous Humboldt University in East Berlin. "People like him started this revolution by opening doors to dissidents." Eppelmann had opened his simple red-brick church to pacifists and ecologists as well as to believers and nonbelievers, to nonconformists and independent thinkers, even to rockers and punks.

Before beginning his theological studies at twenty-six, he had worked as a bricklayer not far from the house where he grew up. Eppelmann explained his conviction that "as a Christian you had to get involved, to oppose injustice, and there was a lot of that here." Early in the 1980s he helped organize a peace movement to oppose the installation of Soviet missiles in East Germany.

Sometimes the police surrounded the church during worship services. But even when they arrested several people who had attended worship and when he had evidence that his telephone was being tapped, Pastor Eppelmann stood firm. The leader of the Democracy Now movement, Werner Wiemann, told a reporter for the *Christian Science Monitor* that the pastor was "crucial for the opposition. We didn't go to church because we were religious. We went because it was the only place to express ourselves." Still, there was an integrity to the space. Often the discussions began with Bible study, conversations for example on the Beatitudes, especially such verses as "Blessed are the peacemakers."

The Rev. Martin Scriba, pastor of St. Paul Church in Schwerin, recalls how significant the free rooms sometimes became. In early September the children's worker at the Lutheran Cathedral, Uta Loheit, had requested official recognition of a grassroots organization called the New Forum Citizens' Initiative. Recognition was denied. On October 2 she wanted members of the New Forum to meet to sign a petition and asked Scriba for the use of the free room at St. Paul Church. He was willing, but the local minister for religious affairs sought to block the use of the church. Nevertheless, a thousand people showed up that evening. In an interview for *The Lutheran*, Scriba explained that under the circumstances he couldn't turn them aside. The meeting led to a demonstration, Leipzig style, on October 23. There was no publicity, but forty thousand people participated, marching to the city's Old Garden. Party officials planned a counter demonstration, also at the Old Garden, and at the same time. So the New Forum simply left the Old Garden, urging the crowd to follow to Pfaffenteich Lake in the center of the city. Most followed. "Like the demonstrations of Martin Luther King, the march had power, but not the power of force," Scriba said. Afterward the marches in Schwerin took place weekly.

On September 8, Bishop Christoph Demke of Magdeburg wrote an open letter to the government leaders. In it he urged all East Germans to begin debating the nation's future after forty years of Communism. He urged the people to decide what to retain, what to reject and what to reform. He called for "an open and courageous discussion about the realities of life." Bishop Demke cited "the contradiction between the conditions that the individual experiences and what he is told in the newspapers." This, he wrote, is "an impertinence that has become unbearable." He told the government officials that "without the courage to tell the painful truth there can be no real growth of trust between governors and governed."

Then on September 10, 1989, the church federation's leadership conference issued a basic statement on the situation in the GDR. The statement took the form of a letter addressed to Erich Honecker, then the party secretary and the chairman of the Council of State. The letter had evolved over a period of weeks and was based in part on what the church leaders had heard in the public discussions and forums that took place in the free rooms. As they moved toward sending the letter to Honecker, the church leaders worked with a theological document prepared by forty-six-year-old Professor Friedrich Schorlemmer of the Wittenberg Seminary. Another major contributor to the dialogue was Heino Falcke, who for two decades had been deeply involved in ecumenical conversations on social theology. He is known among his friends as a strong leader who is "too radical to become a bishop."

The full text of the letter to Honecker follows, both because it was so courageous and because the reforms that

78 *Leadership for Liberation*

were granted two months later substantially followed its recommendations:

> Anxious and concerned, the Leadership Conference of the Evangelical Churches notes that the numbers of people applying for release from GDR citizenship have not diminished, that citizens are leaving the GDR by way of the Hungarian/Austrian border, and that some individuals are trying to force their emigration by other means.
>
> Faced with this situation, the Conference does not know what it can do. Even the easing of travel restrictions, as requested by the Conference, has not helped — in its present scope — to reduce the number of exit applications.
>
> The Conference cannot offer a short-term solution for these problems. We believe a major reason for the exit applications is that changes in the society, which are expected by the people and long overdue, are being refused. We consider it absolutely essential and urgent to start a process in our country which will allow responsible participation by citizens in shaping our social life, ensure productive discussion of the necessary tasks in an open forum, and permit confidence in the work of our organs of state.
>
> Therefore, we are asking urgently and again that steps be taken
>
> - to lead open and true-to-life discussions about the causes of discontent and malfunctions in our society and not to reject them out of hand with stereotypical admonitions or even with threats.
>
> - to accept critical objections by citizens and to give them consideration so that the results will be noticeable changes beneficial to all.
>
> - to work toward making available pertinent information in all political and economic areas and toward realistic reporting by our media which no longer contradicts what our citizens are seeing with their own eyes and experiencing for themselves day after day.

- to see to it that all government offices respect each citizen as a partner who shares responsibility rather than treating him/her as a subject who needs supervision.

- to secure for all citizens, regardless of family ties, permission to travel to other countries.

- to permit officially the return of all GDR citizens who have moved to another country.

The Conference is aware that the solution of the present problems is a lengthy process. In this process, the readiness of other states to negotiate and change, especially that of the Federal Republic of Germany, will also be an important factor. New ideas and different conceptions will be necessary to make it possible to eliminate present tensions and to level out an effectively one-sided economic slope.

The Conference sees it as its main task to consider with its congregations what it means for us as churches that people do not want to stay here with us. The life and actions of Christians must show that they themselves are ready to change and to take responsibility in their society.

The Conference will share this letter with the members of its congregations to encourage them to think about the problems discussed.

The cover letter to the congregations, sent the same day, stated:

For consideration in our churches and for reflection by each individual, the Conference is repeating what it already has said several times before:

We implore you that "you remain in our community and not leave the GDR. Our society needs each person with his/her gifts and potential. It loses diversity, and our country becomes poorer, when people withdraw and leave. Every one who goes away leaves others behind and more alone. . . .

"The church regards it as her obligation to help bring about conditions under which people will gladly live in

our society and will no longer want to apply for release
from citizenship."

In view of the incalculable gaps already opened up in
our health services, in the economy and in other areas, we
must remind you that every person is not only responsible
for shaping his/her own life but also shares responsibility
for the community into which he/she has been placed.

The church had urgently pressed its members and
others not to emigrate. Professor Friedrich Schorlemmer,
a Wittenberg theologian, called the departures "a flight
from responsibility." Those who had shouted "We want
to leave!" however, had begun to act and the trickle
became an exodus. On September 9, the Hungarian government, in response to the appeal of Protestants and
Roman Catholics there, opened the border to Austria and
fifteen thousand crossed the border in three days.

By early October it was clear that something would
have to happen. In the churches there were prayers that
justice would come without violence, and on the evening
of October 2, twenty-five thousand assembled in Leipzig.
The police broke up the demonstration.

There was a show of military force in East Berlin on
October 6 and 7 when the fortieth anniversary of the German Democratic Republic was celebrated. Every attempt
to protest was beaten back by violent interventions of the
Stasi, the secret police. Thousands were mistreated, beaten
by the police or detained in prison. But the guest speaker,
Mikhail Gorbachev, seemed to offer a word of hope in his
ambiguous phrase, "Life itself punishes those who delay."

The next Monday in Leipzig, after services in all five
downtown churches, seventy thousand began marching.
The police and army were ready. So were the hospital
emergency rooms. The Lutheran Bishop, Johannes Hempel, warned of a blood bath. But a group of six men,
including Superintendent Johannes Richter of the Thomas
Church and Kurt Masur, the conductor of the Gewand-

haus Orchestra, convinced those in power not to use violence.

For many East Germans, that day, October 9, was the real turning point: *die Wende*. It became clear that the revolution could be achieved without violence. The tone and the participation in the Leipzig prayer services also had changed. Those who wished to emigrate were outnumbered. An opposition group known as the New Forum had been organized and thousands had taken the dramatic and dangerous step of signing their names and addresses to the membership roll. Pastor Wonneberger of St. Lukas Church was calling for nonviolent resistance to the state. He told people not to carry things that the police believed could become weapons. He also urged them not to resist arrest. At the rally following the service on October 9, the people shouted, *Wir bleiben hier! Wir sind das Volk!* "We want to stay! We are the people!" The turning point already was visible.

Now there were daily demonstrations throughout the republic, nearly always beginning in the churches following the Leipzig model: prayers for justice, calls for nonviolence, candles and "We Shall Overcome." The chairperson of the church federation, Bishop Werner Leich, issued a pastoral letter that was read throughout the German Democratic Republic. "I beg you, friends and fellow citizens," he wrote, "no matter what happens, do not deviate from the principle of nonviolence. Follow the example of Dr. Martin Luther King.... To the members of the security forces, I say: whoever gives the order to beat and injure peacefully demonstrating members of their own people, and those who carry out such an order, must answer for themselves before God and humanity."

His appeal was not merely a plea for nonviolence. He identified himself with the central issue: "Do not let yourselves be intimidated any longer by the thought that speaking the truth could bring you trouble. No renewal in the truth can come about unless we are willing to be

bold and to make sacrifices. God has given us the spirit
of strength.... Love holds the door of reconciliation open
to everyone." The daily demonstrations also echoed the
new, popular slogan: "We are the people!" The Monday
evening vigils drew many who had no ties to the church;
at one a young child was heard to observe, "Mommy, they
don't even know the 'Our Father.'"

The movement picked up speed. On October 18, Erich
Honecker was replaced by Egon Krenz, who declared, almost immediately, that the "socialist society needs and
wants the contribution of all religious citizens. More
unites than divides us." He — like most other East Germans — recognized that the churches, rather than the party
or any other group, had the confidence of the people.
Krenz conferred with church officials as one of his first
acts. That meeting initiated a series of meetings in which
the political leaders seemed to acknowledge that because
of their contacts with *das Volk* the pastors and bishops
could be helpful in a transition.

On October 20, the Dessau churches held the first
service under the theme "Prayer for Renovation." The
Johannes Church was overcrowded and several hundred
people could not get in. On the following Fridays these
services took place in four inner-city churches, the Roman Catholic Peter and Paul Church, the Evangelical
St. Peter's Church and St. George's Church in addition
to the St. John's Church. Planning was done ecumenically
and in each case the worship was a prelude to a peaceful
demonstration of four thousand or more people through
the main streets of the city. Lothar Biener, a lay leader
at St. Peter's congregation, believes that "the combination
of gathering, praying and demonstrating, adapted from
the Leipzig model, is one of the important reasons for
peaceful change. Liberated from decades-long authoritarian rule, from fear and mistrust, we are now aware that as
hardly ever before in history we can exercise influence in
the course of our future."

By the time the democracy movement was spreading through the German Democratic Republic, those who had found their voice in the churches were clear about their goals. According to an Evangelical pastor, Friedrich Schorlemmer, "A new people, a new citizenry [was] born in the demonstrations." On October 31, 1989, which coincided with the anniversary of the Reformation, people from Luther's old Castle Church in Wittenberg marched to the city hall where they tacked seven demands — they called them "Seven Theses" — to the door. Their concrete demands included an end to tampering with letters addressed to persons abroad.

The "Word for the Day," selected months earlier and studied throughout GDR on Reformation Day, was Isaiah 62:10, "Go through, go through the gates. Prepare the way for the peoples; build up, build up the highway, clear it of stones...." As it turned out, the text was as prophetic today as when it was written.

Nearly a million people swarmed into the center of East Berlin on November 4, called together by a coalition of pastors, artists, writers and actors. They demanded freedom of speech and freedom of the press. Between November 3 and November 9 nearly forty-five thousand East Germans had emigrated to the West. At one point, the East German authorities sought to stem the tide of persons who had planned to go West from vacations in Hungary and Czechoslovakia. The officials authorized a special train to cross the GDR and formally "expelled" the refugees. But hordes of young workers blocked the tracks in cities along the way, piling aboard. It was the strongest signal yet.

Then the government published a new travel law, acknowledging the will of the people and hoping that if persons were free to come and go as they pleased, they might go west but then return home. For Gratia and Steven Johns-Boehme, ecumenical co-workers from the National Council of Churches in the U.S.A. assigned to the churches in the GDR, the sight of people freely moving through the Wall to West Berlin was surpassed by the view of long lines of East Berliners returning after a day in the West. "Now," they said, "people could at last remain in their own country without feeling, as one put it, 'incarcerated in a huge concrete prison.'" The traffic, however, was largely westward.

Thus on November 9 the Wall was broken. Germany had experienced the first nonviolent revolution in its history. The following Sunday, Pastor Wonneberger recalled the Old Testament story and told his congregation at St. Lukas Church, "For nine Mondays we marched through the city, and the Wall came tumbling down."

Almost immediately the president of the Federation of Evangelical Churches released a statement expressing appreciation for peaceful activities that had led to the opening of the border. Requesting continued commitment to nonviolent involvement, Bishop Werner Leich said, "Only without violence can we win justice and peace, only without violence can we protect the life entrusted to us. . . . Only the spirit of reconciliation can free us to solve the problems of the present courageously and seize the opportunity for the future." His letter also appealed for free and secret elections, for the establishment of a constitutional system, and for truthfulness in information. In addition he urged that people avoid the spirit of fear and revenge.

By November, there was no functioning government. "Round Table talks" involving all political forces were held to establish a path toward a new government. The churches were the only force with the credibility to call for and chair the talks. The sessions, designed to explore ways to resolve the national crisis, were chaired by Bishop Gottfried Forck of the Evangelical Church of the Union. During those sessions one politician acknowledged the role of the religious organizations: "We have to be clear," he said, "that it was the churches that spoke up for the people over the years and gave them a place to find their voices." In addition to space and shelter, the churches provided a kind of moral authority, urging a global perspective and a nonviolent approach.

A group of eight members of the United Church of Christ were visiting in East Germany during October and November. The Rev. Russell Bennett, of Tulsa, Oklahoma, began to understand what the changes could mean for individuals when a youngster in a family where he was staying returned from school one afternoon to report: "We're not going to be graded in civics anymore." Civics was the name given to the required course of political indoctrination.

The Rev. Frederick A. Wenner, of Frederick, Maryland, was in Wittenberg on November 4. He described how thousands had gathered "within the shadow of Martin Luther's church and just two blocks from the birthplace of the Protestant Reformation." There were at least a million people demonstrating that day in East Berlin. In Wittenberg, "the first of the marchers to step to the microphone was a bearded guitar player who led us in singing 'We Shall Overcome.'"

Wenner went to the Harz mountain region two days later, where an ecumenical prayer service was held in a Roman Catholic church. "Local people of all ages were jammed into the chancel, wedged into every aisle, hanging from the balcony, standing outside the open windows in a cold, drenching rain," he wrote. The eight Americans were staying in various homes the night that the German Democratic Republic opened its borders for the first time to enable its citizens to visit in the West. Dolores Smith, of Hudson, Kansas, spent the evening in a small village where she watched television with a group of students. "They just couldn't believe that it could happen so quickly," she recalls. And later that week, just twenty-four hours after the Wall was opened, Wenner was one of eight hundred worshipers who filled an Evangelical church. After songs and intercessory prayers, an offering was taken for hungry people in the Third World. Then there was a candlelight procession that met a much larger crowd in the town square. "We followed marshals who were wearing 'No Violence' sashes," he recalls. "The strongest applause came when someone went to the microphone to thank the churches for speaking out against government oppression long before others dared to go public with their protests."

Later, in April 1990, the Rev. Alfred Radeloff of Dessau, a city of 104,000 south of Berlin, visited the United Church of Christ's Southern Conference in North Carolina. He explained that the U.S. civil rights movement had had a major impact on the East Germans, who frequently sang "Let My People Go" and "We Shall Overcome" in English. The demonstrations usually began in the churches, where the importance of nonviolence was stressed. To teach the methods of nonviolent social and political change, some of the churches used a film about the life of Dr. Martin Luther King, Jr. At that time, Radeloff noted, "we had no way of knowing how the government would react." They obviously recalled how, during the Prague Spring of 1968, Soviet tanks put an end to "socialism with a human face." He was well aware that the world had changed; youth in both East and West Germany were wearing Gorbachev buttons. But in a tense and uncertain situation, no one is ever sure where demonstrations might lead.

Happily, violence was avoided and East German Pastor Uwe Dittmer, who spent a year in the UCC's Penn Central Conference as a "peace partner," said, "You can't imagine a revolution without hatred and violence. But ours has been connected with joy.... I'm deeply convinced that this revolution is part of the way God is leading his people." East Germans are especially pleased with the fact that the changes were peaceful. The Rev. Helmut Schiewe, of Herrnhut, wrote to American Moravian friends: "We are very impressed and humbled that God used the Evangelical Church in the GDR to see that it would be a revolution without violence."

Radeloff, who is a district superintendent of the Evangelical Church of the Union, compared the forty years under Communist rule to the forty years the children of Israel wandered in the wilderness on their way to the promised land. The churches of Dessau, as in other parts of East Germany, had provided the gathering places for young people and others whose demands for freedom eventually could not be ignored. In the fall of 1989, Radeloff himself had headed a committee to consider the problems of his city and how to work through various problems before freedom could be part of a longer process of renewal. "We preached the right things," he notes reflectively, "and now came the right movement." His reflection was confirmed a thousand times over. One example was Thomas Bonesky, first secretary of the Leipzig Communist Party. In retrospect, he wondered who made the decision on October 9 not to fire on the demonstrators. But he was clear that "the most constructive and responsible force throughout the whole thing was the church." It was hard for a party official, and therefore an avowed atheist, to admit. "I was raised to regard the church as my enemy. I never talked to a pastor in my life, before the Round Table discussions in Leipzig."

A banner spanning a street in that city where the model for peaceful candlelight marches was developed said it all: *Wir danken Dir, Kirche.* "We thank you, Church."

The toppling of the Wall and the changing of the guard in East Germany opened more than the border crossings. Immediately there was talk of the unification of the two Germanies and there were hundreds of issues to be dealt with. Many of the church leaders who had been so deeply involved in the movement now found themselves in different situations. Many faced the question of how deeply to remain involved in the intricate task of creating and negotiating a new social structure. Now there were new kinds of pressures: suddenly the politics of the Federal Republic of Germany swept over East Germans like a tidal wave. They were ill prepared by the years of dictatorship and authoritarian rule. And they also faced the pressure of electoral deadlines. Pressured by economic collapse, the first free elections were moved up from May to March 18, 1990.

As the elections approached, three church leaders moderated the Round Table discussions, which, to preserve neutrality, were first held in the Dietrich Bonhoeffer House. The plenary sessions were chaired in turn by Martin Ziegler, general secretary of the Federation of Evangelical Churches; Karl-Heinz Ducke, director of studies for the Catholic Bishops' Conference; and Martin Lange, pastor of the United Methodist Friedenskirche (Peace Church), who also serves as general secretary of the Association of Christian Churches. The federation made Matthias Reichelt, who directs its office, available to keep the Round Table organization going, including the use of church typewriters and photocopiers. Eventually, the federation released Reichelt completely for the increasingly complicated task.

The Round Table set up a special panel to investigate the crimes of the security police. Bishop Gottfried Forck was named to that panel because of his high credibility. Many pastors were involved in local Round Tables. The experience of church leaders in chairing ecclesiastical meetings made them especially valuable as moderators who often were called on to show considerable patience. Their negotiating skills were strained by the lack of procedural rules and by spontaneous outbreaks of democratic fervor.

The Democratic Awakening Party, along with several other political groups, emerged from the protest movement that had used the churches' free rooms. The Democratic Awakening was led by Rainer Eppelmann, who admitted that he is "a divided man" who really loves his ministry work. "But I cannot turn my back on society," he explains. His secretary is candid: "It is no longer possible for Mr. Eppelmann to serve as a pastor. He has become a speaker for the people." In early February 1990, the pastor who was known for his pacifist views and his initiatives in the peace process, took a leave of absence to serve as a minister without portfolio in the transitional government. After the May elections he took over the Ministry of Disarmament and Defense in the government of Lothar de Maizière — an irony that he was himself quick to point out. At the end of June, Eppelmann formally ended his pastoral duties in a service at which conscientious objectors first barred his way with a chain of "broken dog tags." They protested the support for the East German military that the pastor-turned-politician had announced. In July they called on him to reaffirm his support for the peace movement.

When Eppelmann's Democratic Awakening Party joined the Alliance for Germany dominated by the Christian Democrats before the election, Professor Friedrich Schorlemmer led his more liberal wing of the Awakening Party to join the Social Democratic Party. Martin Kirchner, a lay leader of the Evangelical church, became general secretary of the Christian Democrats. The leader of the more conservative German Social Union is Hans-Wilhelm Ebeling. Ebeling, a Leipzig pastor, frequently speaks of the Christian principles on which his politics are based.

Manfred Stolpe, a lawyer who is president of the Berlin-Brandenburg regional consistory and vice-chairperson of the church federation, was asked first to run for prime minister and then to serve as foreign minister. He rejected both but on October 14, 1990, he was elected as president of the new Brandenburg province. He ran as a Social Democrat. The premier's post was offered in turn to Bishop Forck, Christof Ziemer, church superintendent in Dresden, and to Friedrich Magirius, superintendent in Leipzig. When each declined, de Maizière, a lawyer who was vice moderator of the church federation and a mem-

ber of the Christian Democratic Party, agreed to serve. The
Rev. Markus Meckel was selected as foreign minister, and
the Rev. Hans-Wilhelm Ebeling of Leipzig's St. Thomas
Church became minister for development aid.

Concerns at the Hendrik Kraemer House in West Berlin, a center for ecumenical dialogue, were expressed in
a rally with the theme "Support but don't subdue" East
Germany. Be Ruys, the center's director, was disturbed by
some of the rhetoric in both East and West calling for
"Germany — United Fatherland." She emphatically stated,
"We don't need to return to German arrogance."

In the churches of the former GDR people still speak
of *die Wende*, the turning. But it is no longer a particular
day, a point in time, happy as the memories of those October and November days of nonviolence are. The turning
now is seen as a gradual process by which democracy will
develop and the people will be served by the state.

CHAPTER SEVEN

Czechoslovakia: Divided Churches Unite for Freedom

In Prague and in the cities and towns of Czechoslovakia, the turning from authoritarian rule became known as the "Velvet Revolution." As in Poland and Hungary and East Germany, the revolution happened relatively peacefully: it was soft, like velvet. Because the revolution came after the other three, the snows of November and December had begun to fall: there was a softness and quiet in the streets, like velvet.

But the velvet was not the black velour of ecclesiastical robes. The church was in the front rows but not at center stage, as it had been in Poland and East Germany. On stage were the players and playwrights. Any velvet garments would be from the costume closet of Prague's popular theater, the Magic Lantern, which served as the staging point for the Civic Forum. The dressing rooms backstage furnished the offices for the coalition of activists who played to the crowds with all the skill and flourish of professional actors.

More than in the other nations, the churches in Czechoslovakia were divided and broken, many were dispirited.
Although formally they acknowledged the ecumenical
spirit, both Catholics and Protestants seemed to have been
influenced less by the Second Vatican Council than Christians of other nations. Perhaps the memory of the ruthless
suppression of Protestants during the Counter Reformation and of martyred reformer Jan Hus remained so vivid
that church unity was impossible. The Stalinists had come
closer to breaking the Czech churches than elsewhere, both
at the end of World War II and again after the Prague
Spring of 1968. The regime had denied preaching licenses
to many of the strongest priests and pastors, forcing them
to do manual labor and monitoring them carefully.

Among both Catholics and Protestants, there had been
more compromise than in Hungary, Poland and the
GDR. Even around the aging Catholic primate František Cardinal Tomášek, there were priests whose loyalties
he questioned. They belonged to an organization called
Pacem in Terris, which the Vatican refused to recognize. Protestants were deeply divided following the Prague
Spring. Some still had high hopes for the dialogue
with Marxists that was facilitated by the Christian Peace
Conference. Others raised relatively weak voices in opposition to the hardline government's violations of human
rights. Many Christians witnessed to their faith by quietly
enduring the denial of educational and professional opportunities. Still others were simply dispirited, seemingly
content to worship and to wait.

Among Protestants and Roman Catholics who opposed
the government, the most articulate were those who had
lost their preaching licenses. Some of these had been
signers of Charter 77; for their efforts to support the
Helsinki human rights accords they had been imprisoned
or otherwise disciplined. Those who were not behind bars,
however, continued to press their churches to take more
courageous stands. Two who took considerable risks and

who had suffered significantly were the Rev. Jan Duš and Father Josef Zverina.

In response to the "dissident" clergy, the synodical council of the Evangelical Church of Czech Brethren in 1987 appointed a commission that, before the Velvet Revolution made such actions fashionable, presented a series of recommendations to the government for a revised state constitution. In early 1989 the government appeared somewhat more ready than before to discuss the proposals, which included such statements as:

- Each person has the right to freedom of thought, conscience and religion.
- No pressure should be exerted that would hinder freedom of expression.
- Religious faith should not be a reason to deny a person the right to an education or to any occupation or profession.
- Religious communities should be free to assemble and to engage in useful service, such as care for the elderly, sick and the handicapped.
- Hostilities based on religious faith or atheism should be forbidden.
- Capital punishment should be abolished.
- Cultural policies should not be based on ideology.

As the drama of 1989 began to unfold, the voices of the Protestant churches were heard with increasing frequency. At first their words were scattered. Then, as their spirit returned, they became a courageous chorus. Finally, they were empowered and they began to speak in unison.

The Pentecost of this revolution came like a windstorm on November 17. The clouds had been gathering for some months as students in Prague colleges and universities organized carefully. A leadership group, who called themselves "The Ribbon," used the official youth organization, the SSM, as their base of operation. Through the SSM they obtained government permission to hold a rally on the fiftieth anniversary of the martyrdom of a Czech student who had been murdered by the Nazis. There were speeches and tributes at the Prague cemetery where Jan Opletal was buried. The crowd of students multiplied and their impromptu slogans and chants focused increasingly on the hardline officials of the present government. Then as the rally ended, the crowd began moving down the hill, singing "We Shall Overcome." They marched along the Vltava River and into Narodni Avenue toward historic Wenceslas Square with its towering statue of the "Good King" who had protected his people.

But the storm broke before the students reached their destination. Their chants of "Freedom!" were met by riot police and special anti-terrorist forces. The courageous students were well disciplined: they offered flowers to the police. They placed their candles on the streets and opened their arms. "We are unarmed," they said. "See — our hands are bare." But the police answered with clubs. One student was killed. Many were taken to hospitals.

Word spread quickly. By next morning, students at the Charles University, at the Comenius Faculty and at several other colleges had called a strike. Students from the academies of theatrical and motion picture arts (whose hero Václav Havel three times had been imprisoned for supporting human rights through participation in Charter 77) were joined by groups of actors. The actors' strike closed the theaters to plays and reopened them for political discussions. The actors declared that for Czechs 1989 would be known as the "year of the clubs"; they called for a general strike on November 27. The first of what became a torrent of demands was issued. "Legalize the underground paper *Lidové Noviny*," they insisted.

As word spread through the country and around the world, others joined the students and the actors. By late Sunday several opposition groups — including members of Charter 77 — met in one of the theaters. They agreed on the spot to organize a Civic Forum to speak for all. Their Občanske Fórum began with four of its own demands: The president, Gustáv Husák, must resign. So should the Communist Party leaders, especially those who had collaborated with the Russians in 1968 when the Prague Spring ended so violently. The forum also singled out persons who were responsible for attacking the students and halting other peaceful demonstrations. And it called for the release of prisoners of conscience.

Then, day after day, in the wintry winds people massed in Wenceslas Square, placing candles around the statue of the ancient king. The events were both spontaneous and carefully orchestrated. Václav Havel and the Civic Forum met almost constantly in their dressing room headquarters. They issued press releases, organized a dozen groups and met with factory workers. They modified their plans as government leaders lost ground through indecision. The people responded spontaneously, tearing themselves from their televisions to gather in the historic square of all the people.

The Moravian Church was holding its twelfth synod meeting in Prague on November 17 when word arrived that the police had brutally intervened in the nonviolent student demonstration a few blocks away. The business was interrupted for prayers, after which the synod adopted a letter to Prime Minister Ladislav Adamec, condemning the police action and calling for peaceful dialogue with all representatives of the people looking toward the introduction of democratic procedures in the country.

In another part of Prague the Evangelical Church of Czech Brethren also was holding its synod. In response to the police action, the moderator, Dr. Josef Hromádka, attempted unsuccessfully to communicate directly with the government. The Synod sent a message to the churches urging members "not to be afraid to express your opinions." The message, which cited such Czech heros as

St. Cyril and St. Methodius, Jan Hus, Jan Amos Comenius and T. G. Masaryk, also called on members to "support the transformation of our society in the spirit of a convincing social justice and full democracy, which are especially close to our Christian traditions."

Specifically, the message stated: "No one must be allowed to assume power at the cost of others. Precisely these days we have had the first-hand experience of seeing how dreadfully power can be abused. We defend the right of all to assemble and disseminate ideas by nonforceful means. We expect that prisoners of conscience shall be set free. We believe that all of this will lead to a purification and strengthening of our society as a whole rather than to destabilization. This will permit the creation of an atmosphere of mutual trust which is one of the prerequisites for the true establishment of rapprochement and peace throughout the world." Several days later, on November 21, Dr. Hromádka met with Prime Minister Adamec, asking him to halt the brutality. Adamec promised to do so and called the Department of the Interior. Nevertheless, the students of the church's Comenius Faculty of Protestant Theology joined the student strike, which continued until January 4.

The United Methodist superintendent of Prague, J. Cerveňák, wrote to all congregations immediately after the November 17 "massacre," stating that "on both humanistic and Christian grounds I disagree with the beating of helpless people in a bloody manner," and calling on "all Christians to pray for their nation and for a peaceful resolution of the situation." Ten days later the leaders of the Methodist Church took part in a peaceful demonstration and then adopted a declaration approving the principles of the Civic Forum and calling for the abolition of the state's supervision of the churches.

The Methodist leaders also said, "We are aware that democratic freedom implies a great obligation. It is necessary for us to learn to live in freedom. The attainment of new structures does not yet resolve the spiritual struggle." They expressed confidence that the message of the gospel, "which leads to penitence, forgiveness and love, and which creates new relations among people," will be of help "during the new orientation of life in our country."

The Baptist Union also met to express "support of the initiative undertaken by the students, artists and all progressive people in connection with events of November 17." The Baptist believers adopted a seven-point message to the government calling for freedom of speech and the press, the abolition of the laws curtailing the activities of the churches, pastoral care to believers in the military, alternatives to military service for conscientious objectors, the possibility for missionary work and for charitable assistance at home and overseas and specifically for a new government based on political pluralism.

The patriarch of the Czechoslovak Hussite Church also expressed support for the democratic process immediately after November 17. The Hussites' Central Council then met in early December and formulated "certain requirements concerning the coexistence of the church and the state." These included the access of ministers to, and the use of the Bible and religious literature in, social institutions, the army and the prisons. They also called for opportunities for religious education in the Scout movement.

The leadership of the Old Catholic Church issued a statement that urged people to avoid "malicious delight" in blaming others, and also to "atone for many a thing by changing our thinking." The Old Catholic Church sent contributions from its peace fund and from special collections to help meet the needs of striking students. The Orthodox Church in Czechoslovakia issued a statement saying that "in the name of the love of our country, we oppose violence, malice, hatred, and especially fanaticism at the root of which is the effort to enforce upon others one's own political or religious convictions."

Similarly, the churches that are indigenous to Silesia and Slovakia issued statements. The Silesian Evangelical Church of the Augsburg Confession acknowledged that when "our entire society is resolving piled-up problems," many unresolved problems remain within the church. It cited especially the "mistakes made by the church leadership in the past" as well as the need for "a thorough rehabilitation of those adversely affected."

At the beginning of December the Slovak counterpart of the Czech Civic Forum was constituted in the Slovak Evangelical Church of the Augsburg Confession. During two decades in which democratic principles in the churches were suppressed, the situation in that church became unsatisfactory to members. The students and faculty of the Slovak Evangelical Faculty began calling for unlimited freedom of assembly within the church, as well as access to religious literature and a consistent respect for religious freedom.

As the churches began to speak with a common voice, they grew increasingly close together. Father Václav Malý, who had been banned by the government for his participation in Charter 77, was at the center of the Civic Forum and often addressed the crowds along with Havel and Radim Palouš, a prominent and activist Roman Catholic lay person. On November 25, Father Malý appeared on a balcony overlooking the great Square of St. Wenceslas. The crowd had roared its welcome to Alexander Dubček, whose return to public view provided a breath of spring in November. Then Malý invoked the name of the ninety-year-old Cardinal Tomášek. More cheers. Malý read a message from the cardinal: "I thank all those who are fighting for the good of us all and I trust completely the Civic Forum which has become a spokesman for the nation. The Catholic Church stands entirely on the side of the people in their present struggle." The demonstration ended as three hundred thousand people shook their key rings; the sound was unforgettable.

The next day there was a festive mass at the cathedral near Hradcany Castle where the Central Committee of the Communist Party was meeting, torn with dissension. The mass was a celebration of the canonization in Rome two weeks earlier of Agnes of Bohemia, the daughter of a thirteenth-century king who renounced her inheritance to serve the poor. Protestants and Catholics alike recalled the ancient promise that when Agnes was recognized as a saint, miracles would happen in Bohemia. A national television audience and the second vast crowd in as many days heard Cardinal Tomášek urge: "Let us all, wherever we are, fulfill Christ's call, 'You will be my witnesses.' In this grave hour of struggle for truth and justice in our country, the Catholic Church and I are with the nation. We remember Christ's words, 'Blessed are those who hunger and thirst for justice, for they shall have their fill.' None of us can remain uninvolved when the future of our nation is at stake. I beg of you in these days — unite courage to wisdom and refuse violence."

Václav Benda, a Catholic who was one of the original leaders of Charter 77, began work on a blueprint for the new Czechoslovakia. Josef Hromádka, who was also president of the Ecumenical Council of Churches, played a major role in developing the successful strategies of the Civic Forum. During a rally in Wenceslas Square on November 23, the evangelical theologian urged the crowds not to lose sight of Christian values in their search for meaningful lives. He spoke of the great damage that had been done to the environment and to human relations; he urged the crowed to embrace a new lifestyle in which material wealth plays a less significant role.

Among Roman Catholics, a so-called Group of 73 had been meeting since October, planning ways to regain control of the People's Party. Once staunchly Catholic, the party had been brought under the Communist domination by a collaborator-priest, Josef Plojhar. Eleven days after the November 17 "massacre," the Group of 73 accused the neo-Stalinist leaders of the party of collaboration. On November 28, they were successful in their efforts, and Richard Sacher, a close associate of Father Malý, was named general secretary of the People's Party. Sacher and Josef Bartoncik were outspoken in their support of the goals of the Civic Forum.

Eventually, the discredited leaders of the Communist Party Central Committee resigned, and on Sunday, December 10, the UN's Human Rights Day, a new government was sworn in. The enormously popular Havel, after wavering about accepting a political role, was elected president. Dubček was named to chair the Federal Assembly. Father Malý declined a political role. The eloquent priest explained that after having been banned for eleven years, he wanted to work as a priest; on December 17 he began serving at St. Margaret's Basilica. Many believe that eventually he will succeed Tomášek.

Dr. Hromádka was named deputy prime minister with responsibility for culture, education and religion. He accepted the role only after receiving assurance from Cardinal Tomášek and Protestant leaders that they would welcome his decision. The Ecumenical Council announced that it believed that "this serious step taken by a church representative who has decided to enter the sphere of political activity will facilitate, in the new situation, the assertion of all the positive forces that sincerely desire to co-create a society based on the principles of true democracy."

Ironically, one of Dr. Hromádka's first official acts was a trip to Rome, where he invited Pope John Paul II to visit Czechoslovakia as soon as possible. Hromádka's trip also paved the way for renewing diplomatic relations between Czechoslovakia and the Vatican and the naming of Catholic bishops to sees that had been vacant for up to twenty-eight years. The pope agreed to accept the invitation, with the visit to include ecumenical events, but only after Pacem in Terris, the two-hundred-member organization of priests who had collaborated with the Communist government, was dissolved.

Another deputy prime minister, Ján Čarnogurský, a Roman Catholic lawyer, had played a leading role in the church's resistance to the government. Arrested in August 1989 in Bratislava on charges of "subversion" and "incitement," Čarnogurský had been active in Charter 77. Pavel Klener became minister of health and Francis Reindell was also named as a deputy prime minister. Both of them are prominent Roman Catholic lay persons.

At about the time that Hromádka went to Rome, the new government announced that the secretariat for church affairs would be closed and that state supervision of churches would be ended. Licenses would no longer be needed by priests and ministers. By Christmas time, the churches had regular access to the mass media and Czech Christians raised money for food and other supplies that they were permitted to send to Romania. On New Year's Eve an ecumenical service was telecast during which representatives of all the churches participated together.

In the end, the ecumenical spirit seems to have been revived, along with political freedoms. During the papal trip in April 1990, John Paul II talked about the rehabilitation of Jan Hus, the reformer who was burned at the stake as a heretic in 1415, nearly one hundred years before Luther initiated the Protestant Reformation. In July 1990, a fifty-seven-year-old Roman Catholic lay person, Jan Janousek, blamed the Communists for blocking the impact of the Second Vatican Council. Janousek, who had served a prison term for his religious activities, mentioned Jan Hus in a conversation with Peter Steinfels of the *New York Times*. "We've always been unorthodox, a thinking people who don't take everything for granted," he said. "Every Czech, even if he's a Catholic, has a bit of Hussite in him."

CHAPTER EIGHT

Romania:
The Pastor/Prophet
Was the First Hero

As the so-called Velvet Revolution swept across Central and Eastern Europe it seemed that nothing could affect the brash and brutal regime of Romania's President Nicolae Ceausescu. He was tough. He was arrogant. He was ruthless. It was almost as though he taunted the world to a game of King of the Hill. Finally, when people took to the streets to demand a change, the response of the security and paramilitary forces was bloody. But the impossible happened; the last of the hardline dictators had gone too far; the people's anger suddenly surpassed their fear; Ceausescu lost the challenge. Just before Christmas Nicolae Ceausescu and his wife, Elena, ran for their lives. They lost that race, too, and after a hasty trial were executed by a vengeful firing squad.

For more than a quarter of a century Ceausescu had created a powerful base with a puppet party, an ever-loyal Securitate force and tough bodyguards. The dictator had permitted no opposition and cared little for the people.

They seemed resigned to their fate. Once, when bread was in especially short supply, a worker is supposed to have said, "At least they haven't hanged us yet!" The dictator's only goal was to drive his nation to become a model of a Communist planned society. He dreamed of a proud four-thousand-room palace that would shade even the royal houses of the Habsburgs. He cut a swath through the city for a broad boulevard, destroying churches, national treasures and hundreds of homes.

To make way for his "planned cities" he was ready to bulldoze seven thousand villages — beginning with those that housed the nation's ethnic minorities. These included thousands of Hungarian-speaking residents of Transylvania, a region that had been ceded to Romania by the Trianon Treaty of 1920. The villagers were to be housed in "official living centers" where, the policymakers hoped, they would lose their sense of identity as part of a grand scheme of "systematization and modernization" and "homogenization."

Ceausescu kept a tight rein on the whole country, including its churches. His department of religious affairs was involved in every decision affecting the churches. Only recognized religious bodies were permitted to meet publicly. The department closely supervised eleven Christian groups in addition to the Romanian Orthodox Church, which claims more than 70 percent of the population as members. The government office set the times and the frequency of worship services. It had veto power over every religious appointment, sometimes even placing a pastor or priest in a particular congregation. Building permits were seldom issued. Uncooperative pastors and leaders were frequently harassed, sometimes jailed, occasionally beaten. Neither the state radio nor the official television had any time for the churches. Travel to world assemblies was limited and speeches were cleared in advance. The enormous pressures were designed to break the will of every pastor and every church leader.

That strategy almost succeeded. Over the years, bishops, priests and even a patriarch did the dictator's bidding, revealing little or nothing of the bitterness that the people felt nor of any discomfort in their own roles. Unlike the Christian leaders in other Central and Eastern European nations, church officials in Romania showed neither courage nor conviction. In fact, they fawned over the man so many hated. As late as August 1989, on a national holiday, Hungarian Reformed, Roman Catholic and Orthodox leaders sent a telegram affirming Ceausescu's twenty-five-year rule. According to their message, the dictator had "taken the Romanian people to the highest level of civilization." They glorified him as the "most popular son of our nation," the "greatest hero" in Romanian history. Not infrequently, such words of adulation were inserted in reports of speeches by the Securitate after they were delivered by church leaders. Similar language appeared in church documents printed in state-operated publishing houses.

The Orthodox Patriarch Teoctist, who was appointed with the president's approval, agreed to the demolition of many churches — twenty-three in Bucharest alone — to make way for socialist construction projects. The patriarch also ordered the birthdays of the Ceausescus printed in church calendars. Therefore the relatively modest changes in language that were noticeable by the end of the year were themselves revolutionary. People no longer spoke of their former rulers by name; Nicolae and Elena Ceausescu were simply referred to as "the Dictator."

In a later report to the World Council of Churches, the Reformed pastor whose effective ministry and quiet courage ignited the revolution explained that "there was a refusal to present the true conditions of churches in Romania and a pretension that in our country everything is fine, [and that] the churches perform their mission in peace and freedom. This mischaracterization," said László Tökés, "gave birth to a gross misconception which for decades defined the impression abroad of our churches and of Romania. Practically all well-known public personalities and church organizations abroad — including the World Council of Churches — fell victim to this false impression."

Tökés said that "Romanian church authorities, opportunistic and collaborating bishops and preachers of ecumenism succeeded in misleading their sister churches and public opinion in exactly the same fashion that the Ceausescu regime deceived the international diplomatic community." He said that the "international representatives of the churches in Romania were deeply intertwined with the state policy structure, and under the label of ecumenism successfully represented the direct interests of an inhuman, ungodly and oppressive regime — all at the expense of their own believers."

Tökés, an ethnic Hungarian, developed a very successful congregation while serving in a small, mountain village in Transylvania. Worship services were popular. Young people became active participants in the congregation. The young pastor wrote plays that were produced locally, plays that raised issues of Hungarian identity and criticized government policy. Soon he was a marked man, and the security forces prevailed on Bishop László Papp to move Tökés to another parish where he could be watched. Then for eight long years Tökés served as pastor of the Reformed Church in Timisoara, an industrial city located in western Romania one hundred miles from the Hungarian border. During that time the youthful preacher wrote articles and organized protests against the government's systematic repression of its Hungarian minority. Though he was popular with his congregation, it seemed to Tökés that no one in the world heard his pleas. No one, that is, except the hated Securitate. Eventually the courage of the thirty-seven-year-old minister so threatened the powerful seventy-one-year-old dictator that Ceausescu took action. The Securitate first asked that Tökés be excommunicated, but Bishop Papp declined, agreeing however to suspend the pastor from his ministry.

But Tőkés decided to leave Timisoara only if physically forced to do so. On December 17, 1989, as the pressure mounted and threats increased, two hundred members of the Reformed congregation supported their pastor, ringing the parsonage and the church in a human chain to protect Tőkés and his family. Hour by hour the crowd grew, lighting candles, praying, refusing to move. Eventually the ethnic Hungarians were joined by Romanian Orthodox believers, Baptists, Hungarian Catholics, Serbs and German Lutherans; there were five thousand people in the streets around the church.

"It was a qualitative change," Tőkés said. "The solidarity demonstration for me changed into a general protest against the regime. The people cried out, 'Down with Ceausescu,' 'We want liberty!' As the crowd moved toward the center of the city, it grew to fifty thousand. The Securitate, the police, the army and the militia all responded, using tear gas and batons, shields, helmets, rifles and small tanks. The revolution had begun." As the people of Timisoara demonstrated, their numbers continued to swell. A massacre followed. Some estimates of the death toll reached as high as thirty-five hundred. The events in Timisoara ignited demonstrations in other cities, including Bucharest. The people finally had had enough.

With units of the Romanian army called to the church, Tőkés, his wife and her brother climbed a ladder from their home and slipped into the church to await their fate. The pastor stood at the communion table, wearing the black clerical cape that Hungarian preachers use. After first refusing to use their weapons on the crowd that had gathered around the church, the soldiers opened fire and many died. The army then broke into the church and arrested Tőkés after punching him and his wife, who was seven months pregnant. The Tőkéses were carried off to the remote village of Menyö, where they arrived a few days before Christmas. The house to which the Tökéses were taken was surrounded by police twenty-four hours a day. Searchlights turned nights into days. Wolf hounds were brought in and a telephone line was strung to the village that previously did not even have a bus line. For three days the courageous pastor was interrogated repeatedly. The Securitate used psychological torture to force an admission that he was responsible for the violence in Timisoara. A confession would have led to a show-trial with an almost certain sentence of death.

What happened, however, was that the government's action had triggered a national movement in which Romanians as well as ethnic Hungarians stood together and called for the end of the Ceausescu regime. In retrospect, Tökés says, "One of my eyes cries, the other laughs. We must cry for the victims. We cry for those who cry. But I rejoice with those who rejoice. I especially rejoice that Romanians and Hungarians are not separated by hatred and anger but came together first around the church and then in Bucharest. I was especially thrilled when I looked out the window of our home and heard that crowd singing the famous Romanian folk song, the Hora of Unity."

With the dictator gone, there was greater candor. The Holy Synod of the Romanian Orthodox Church admitted that it had often lacked "the courage of martyrs." Before retiring to a remote Orthodox monastery, Patriarch Teoctist acknowledged his "personal guilt." A Lutheran bishop, himself terminally ill, issued a pastoral letter confessing his complicity. "Far too often we did not acknowledge injustice for what it was," Bishop Albert Klein wrote. "We are stricken by the irresponsible use of power and the injustice caused, and by the unnumberable dead and those who mourn for them." Tökés' superior, Bishop Papp, fled the country, taking refuge with his son who lives in Metz, France. Papp attempted to defend his actions, quot-

ing Romans 13 that Christians are bound to obey civil
authorities.

Unlike the other peoples of the region, Romanians won
their freedom only with great losses. Even in the months
after the execution of Ceausescu, Pastor Tökés and his
wife were forced into hiding; progress toward democracy
was slow and, in some ways, inconclusive. Tökés himself
was elected a bishop to succeed László Papp and also was
named to the Council of National Salvation, a coalition
that is seeking stability for the land that continues to experience turmoil and pain. He regards his most urgent role
as working for reconciliation between ethnic factions that
still are struggling with one another. Ceausescu had encouraged the latent and entrenched bigotry to divide and
conquer his own people. After the dictator's death, Tökés
cited emerging anti-Semitism and attacks on gypsies, as he
spoke of plans to establish a House of Reconciliation in
Timisoara.

The pastor who had become a national hero was critical of the role that church leaders had played during
the years of brutality. Nevertheless he affirmed that "the
church and its congregations remained the last refuge of
the oppressed people, deprived of their human rights and
cast into misery. The churches," he said, "remained the
'mighty fortresses' of the 'meek and infirm.' The churches
became the guardians of evangelical, historical, traditional
and human values." The faith of the Romanian people was
demonstrated six months after the Romanian revolution
by thousands of people who knelt in the streets as the
bells rang in memory of those who had died. There was
a steady procession of people carrying wreaths to the center of the Bucharest square that student demonstrators had
designated as a "Communist Free Zone." As hundreds of
candles were lit, people made the sign of the cross. Similar
memorial services were held in towns and villages across
Romania, especially in the Cemeteries of Heroes where the
martyrs of the revolution are buried.

Tökés told the Central Committee of the World Council of Churches that while they were "struggling with internal and external circumstances" the churches "drew strength from their faith and kept alive in the people the hope of liberation." He said the churches became the repository of a better and more just future. "The church was the only institution, organized community or potential opposition force that survived the downfall of the monolithic one-party state," Tökés pointed out. From his own Calvinist tradition, Tökés explained the view that "since the Communist system left no credible leadership in its wake," the church was predestined "to assume a role...representing the genuine interests of the people and maintaining the lasting standards of evangelism and humanitarianism."

Six months after the fall of Ceausescu, the people expressed a mixture of determination and despair. The Rev. Robert C. Lodwick, a U.S. Presbyterian who works in Geneva, visited Romania as part of an ecumenical delegation. He reported not only that the economy was in shambles with long lines waiting for meat and other necessities, but that many people from the old regime were still in positions of responsibility in the new National Salvation Front. An estimated 60 percent of the dreaded Securitate were still functioning. Student demonstrations seeking greater freedoms had been violently disrupted by miners with picks who many assumed were Securitate ("who ever saw miners with clean finger nails?"). On March 19, 1990, there were bloody attacks on ethnic Hungarians in the region around Tirgu Mures.

The lack of trust in the new government, the continuing ethnic strife and the almost total lack in democratic experience or traditions has created tense and difficult circumstances, even within the churches. On the basis of his conversations Lodwick thinks that many believers understand why their church leaders were forced to compromise with the Communist regime and are grateful

that the church survived at all. One sign of hope among
the churches is the renewal of theological education. Enrollment at the Reformed seminary in Cluj has jumped
from the eight new students permitted by Ceausescu each
year to sixty-two in 1990. Fifty-four new students joined
the faculty of theology after the revolution. The dramatic
change is evident in graffiti in prominent places in the
capital: *Jos Comunismul!* "Down with Communism!" *Jos
Cenzura!* "Down with censorship!" *Revolutia Continua!*

The ecumenical Round Table held in June led to the
establishment of an ongoing National Ecumenical Platform designed to keep the dialogue among the churches
alive and furnish a way in which they can speak on public
issues with a united voice. In the face of massive pollution, which threatens the health of many citizens, the
churches also have agreed to work on environmental issues
together. They also recognize the great needs of orphans,
the disabled and the elderly. With the encouragement of
Christians from elsewhere in Europe and from the World
Council of Churches, Romanian church leaders are taking steps toward helping their society resolve its enormous
problems. Many Romanians seem to agree that the nation
needs a second, peaceful revolution. Yet, as Lodwick observes, after forty years of dictatorship people have to learn
even how to begin a dialogue. The ecumenical role of the
churches will be critical in the next several years.

CHAPTER NINE

Why the Churches Did What They Did

Some commentators already are saying that the changes that took place in 1989 were of unprecedented scope. Certainly Europe had not seen such broad strokes on the political canvas since the fall of the Third Reich and the partition of the continent. The decolonization of Africa and Asia affected more people but also extended over a longer period.

As important as the role of the churches was in the democracy movement in Central and Eastern Europe, they would not claim full credit. There was a readiness for change — even in the Kremlin. It was as though beneath the surface of a dormant volcano the pressures had built until change erupted with incredible speed and power. That metaphor, however, fails to capture the generally peaceful way this change emerged from multiple centers.

Nevertheless, it is appropriate to ask how it happened that the churches provided such distinctive and acceptable leadership. Although everyone was surprised by the fast pace and broad success of the movement, what occurred did not take place overnight. Generally speaking, the churches did what they did because they were churches:

They acted out of their faith and their traditions. Their actions were guided by their theology and shaped by their relationships. Their organization and leaders were in place and functioning; more than any other institution in their societies, they controlled the use of their own buildings. And, for all of these reasons, the leadership of the churches was accepted by the people.

During the twentieth century, the churches of the region had developed a keen sense of justice and peace based on biblical teachings. They had experienced the anguish of two World Wars fought on the soil of their own countries. Before and during World War II some of the church leaders in the German Democratic Republic had studied under Dietrich Bonhoeffer, and many of the church officials in Central and Eastern Europe had sought to witness in their own situations according to Bonhoeffer's description of "the church for others." Except in Romania, the churches were deeply influenced by a theology of servanthood.

In several countries, the churches knew only too well the horror of Hitler's concentration camps and extermination centers. Following the Second World War they had experienced the deep continental rift created by ideological differences. In the midst of such pain and isolation, the churches had found the strength to stand for wholeness and to speak of hope. Living under very difficult circumstances their identities had been based in large part on memories; they had helped to preserve national heritages despite the enforced overlay of political relationships that looked east to the Soviet Union rather than west to the other nations of Europe. They had emphasized national traditions, including the recognition of earlier patriots and saints who had made substantial sacrifices for their homelands.

The churches also represented and articulated an ecumenical worldview. Their ties to Christians in other parts of the world had provided opportunities for travel, for helpful conversations and for the setting of agendas that looked beyond production goals or military objectives. Protestant and Orthodox Christians enjoyed these ecumenical relations in the context of the World Council of Churches. Roman Catholics traced their commitment to ecumenism to the documents of the Second Vatican Council.

The churches' role in the democracy movement was, therefore, based on their own theological and institutional integrity. People of faith now affirm that the Spirit of the living God emboldened and encouraged the churches of Central and Eastern Europe. Without denying that affirmation, it may also be said that, generally speaking, the churches represented the people. They were able, to a remarkable degree, to speak to the government authorities on behalf of the people. They had done this, except in Romania, in ways that had won the respect of the masses without breaking their contacts with the governments.

In ways not fully understood, the churches in each of these nations had been prepared by their faith and their history to live in the midst of difficulty without being overwhelmed by it. Their shared sense of hope and their courageous commitment to reconciliation determined their style and their goals as well as their direct involvement.

Part III

Hopes and Fears

We carry no bitterness in our hearts, because as followers of Jesus, we have forgiven.

—Uwe Holmer, director of the church-
sponsored retirement home in Lobetal, Germany

CHAPTER TEN

The New Order

The Anxiety of Change

Concern over the pace of change was expressed by the Rev. Wolfgang Steckel of Dessau. During the demonstrations last fall and winter, according to the Evangelical pastor, many people were concerned that change would happen so fast that anarchy or at least disorientation would result. "We have to keep order," they were saying, "and the state party (SED) had experience in ruling the country." The opposition groups and parties have quarrels with the programs and the leadership, Steckel explained to his American friends at Immanuel United Church of Christ in Hartford, Connecticut. "It is not easy to create a party on the point of zero, with no traditions, no experience, no technical means and no money. And furthermore, the citizens have no experience in democracy or in the electoral process." Steckel recalls that the last democratic republic in his part of Germany existed between 1918 and 1933. "It was a bad time with unemployment and inflation. So we are very anxious about what will happen."

The Rev. Günter Krusche, the general superintendent for the East Berlin churches, used the image of the locks along a canal to describe his similar worries. "If the gates are opened too quickly, or on both sides at the same time,

all are in imminent danger." People were leaving and, with
the changes in government, his fears seemed well founded.
During the summer of 1990 it became clear that crimi-
nal elements quickly step in to fill vacuums created when
authorities change. The East Berlin newspaper *Berliner Zei-
tung* reported on July 19 that in the first six months of
1990 twice as many people were robbed as in the same
period the year before. Attacks on foreigners and other activities of right-wing radicals (such as the desecration of
cemeteries and the call of "Heil Hitler!") also increased.
The paper stated that neo-fascist groups from West Germany and Austria had some success in creating right-wing
organizations in Berlin, Leipzig, Cottbus and Halle, all in
the former German Democratic Republic. Concerned for
ethics and morals — as well as painfully mindful of the
past — the churches began to ask how they could help
resolve that situation.

Few persons, inside the churches or within the governments or military, expected that change could come
so quickly. There was a readiness — or rather an eager-
ness — for change. Still, political shifts of the magnitude
experienced in so short a time during the fall and winter of 1989–90 probably never had come before without
violence. The pace of change, which the new president of
Czechoslovakia Václav Havel described as "the accelerating
pace of history," left people physically and intellectually
breathless. The demise of Communist governments was
followed by urgent and hasty efforts to resolve long-seated
economic problems. While patience was clearly very thin
in the face of empty bread shelves and the prospect of
widespread unemployment, the solutions are agonizingly
complex and cannot be resolved by mass demonstrations
or the rhetoric of freedom. Many of the new leaders were
themselves anxious that the impatience of hungry people
would somehow be ignited and the progress that had been
gained without violence lost in a moment of passion.

The churches are hardly prepared to provide definitive

leadership, especially when they themselves are so economically vulnerable. Their "free rooms" are no longer needed as places where shared visions can lead to the development of practical strategies. Now everything is free, and nothing is free. The emerging task of the churches is to encourage the people to review various economic models and to seek constructive goals within the context of a new Europe, a family of nations that brings together the best of historic national identities and in which members are encouraged to assist one another.

The anxieties created by urgent, seemingly insoluble, economic problems were only part of Central and Eastern Europe's collective headache on the morning after the Wall was breached. Suddenly, the artificial props are gone and individuals and groups are faced with the task of creating new social structures on virtually nonexistent, or at best weak, foundations. Those tasks often seem overwhelming to church leaders and others who are in a position to see the situation in a broad perspective. Some of the issues that the churches are facing are described below.

When the Pressure Is Off

It was one thing for Christians and their churches to deal with the problems created by governments that officially had promoted atheism. In a sense, the "enemy" was clearly identifiable and, as such, the churches developed a common if not unified approach. It was important just to maintain the faith and to continue to hold worship services as an act of faith. Christian families had an added incentive to teach religious values in their homes. The subtle persecution that came through limits on educational and career development was seen by many as a sacrifice for their convictions. Now, however, the churches of Central and Eastern Europe face what is perhaps a more difficult problem: Western-style secularism that is both faceless and ever-present.

Janusz Narzynski, the Lutheran bishop in Warsaw, says that secularism is growing rapidly in the new Poland. "We say we are a Christian nation," Narzynski explains, "but we find paganism among us. This is not a result of years of official Marxist ideology. That had little effect on us. Rather we find a growing secularism."

In Poland today up to 40 percent of the nation's 100,000 Lutherans attend church each Sunday at some 122 parishes and 199 preaching points. Bishop Narzynski believes that his church's greatest challenge is "building a quality of hope rather than filling church buildings." He is working at this with 103 pastors while 50 students are in seminary preparing for the ministry. Until now, at least, the secular impact on the Roman Catholic Church in Poland has not been publicly discussed. In any case, the expectation of attendance at Sunday Mass has never been as strong in European parishes as it once was in the United States.

The secular trend described by Bishop Narzynski has been noticed elsewhere in Central and Eastern Europe. Members of a confirmation class in the German Democratic Republic recently were asked about "other gods." The flannel board in their Vogtland classroom had images and words to remind the young students of Buddha, Apollo and idols in wood and stone. During one class session the pastor told the class how he had grown up at a time when many Germans expressed great pride in Marxism, atheism and *Gottlosigkeit*, godlessness. Then he asked the young people to identify the gods of the GDR. They made a list. "Money, auto, moped-motor bike, power, Hitler with power, sports, work, entertainment, houses." The Rev. Herbert Brokering, who teaches at Luther Northwestern Seminary in St. Paul, Minnesota, described his visit to Vogtland in an article in *The Lutheran*. He wrote about how the class discussed the commandment, "You shall have no other gods before me."

The students told about school teachers who were ill because their faith in atheism has been undermined. The confirmation class talked about evidences of secularism that are close to home: drugs, alcohol, superstition and luck. They told Brokering, "a false god is what becomes most essential to me." The pastor of the Vogtland church believes that "our people must learn to speak their own faith, to express themselves." Some walls, he says, are invisible; and he is convinced that it is harder to tear down invisible walls than to break through those you can see. "The *Mauer*, the wall, is within us," he told Brokering. "It has made us quiet; it has closed our mouths." This pastor believes that the place of liberation is the church, worship, church council rooms and catechetical classes.

The consequences of this secular trend have been especially noted in the churches of the former GDR, which during 1989 were often filled by activists who utilized the free rooms and who gathered before the demonstrations for candlelit services. Four months after the Wall was opened, Billy Graham took a preaching crusade to East Berlin. He drew only ten thousand persons rather than the one hundred thousand predicted. A service in Gethsemane Church, which often had three thousand persons present for the Monday evening demonstrations, drew only eight hundred persons. A typical Sunday service draws fewer than one hundred. The pastor, the Rev. Elisabeth Eschner, explained this waning interest as "the experience of our times." Billy Graham's experience has been matched in many local congregations.

Werner Kraetschell explained this circumstance when he said, "Churches no longer are the island where people can find freedom. We are only one among many equal groups." Enrollment for courses at the Evangelical Academy in East Berlin has dropped markedly since the Wall was opened. One West German pastor, the Rev. Hans

Joachim Curth, suggested that "Now the people of East Germany are experiencing West German conditions."

Western secularism, however, probably is not solely to blame. At least one survey suggests that forty years of leadership by avowed atheists in the GDR took a serious toll in the belief patterns. A poll conducted in early 1990 by the Institute for Public Opinion discovered a wide discrepancy between residents of the German Democratic Republic and the Federal Republic of Germany in response to the question, "How important is God in your life?" In the FRG, 10 percent responded "completely unimportant," while 42 percent gave the same reply in the GDR. The institute, which is based in the Federal Republic, explained this by asserting that "the forty-year division of East and West Germany left its mark on the religious views of Germans."

Church membership is significantly higher in the West, where 85.6 percent are at least nominally members, according to the same survey, although church attendance there is very low. Only about 33 percent of residents of the former GDR identified themselves with the church. Membership and support for the churches there were voluntary. In the Federal Republic, church taxes are collected from those who have not taken the initiative to cancel their membership. (Such membership cancellations have been running about 140,000 annually in recent years.)

Interchurch cooperation is another area in which changes may take place now that the pressures imposed on the religious institutions by Communist governments have been eased or eliminated. The impulse to work together ecumenically was in part the development of a coalition for self-defense. When the churches no longer are being persecuted, or when a united front is no longer needed, churches tend to focus more on their own denominational identities and programs. By the summer of 1990 the unity forged during 1989 already was showing some signs of falling apart.

Partly to counter this centrifugal effect on the democracy movement, the representatives of four Romanian churches are seeking to establish a "national ecumenical platform." When they met in June 1990, leaders of Romanian Orthodox, Reformed and Lutheran churches agreed "the churches, whose identity is often linked with national identity, have a special responsibility to help reduce tension and create positive models of a multi-racial, multicultural society." They candidly agreed that the minority churches in Romania need to clarify their own positions in dialogue with the Romanian Orthodox Church. According to the church leaders, who agreed to meet again in 1991, the primary task facing the churches is "to help build trust and confidence" among the people of Romania so that "freedom and democracy can be fully achieved through nonviolent and reconciliatory means." This is the task to which László Tökés has committed his own ministry.

In Czechoslovakia, the Protestant churches have expressed concern over what they regard as links that are "too close" between their new government and the Roman Catholic Church. During an extraordinary meeting of the Conference of European Churches held in Geneva in May 1990, Pavel Smetana, deputy moderator of the Evangelical Church of Czech Brethren, reported that he had been prompted to write to the pope shortly before the pontiff's 1990 visit to Czechoslovakia. Smetana told the pope that "clouds appear on the horizon of social life and raise anxiety in the minds of all Christians longing for unity." He asked the pope, "Will the period of our newly won freedom be the time of God... in which we will be able to penetrate even deeper into the unity of faith, love and hope? Or will national freedom lead to a new fission and to a division when each church will push through its own interests, led by the instinct of self-preservation." He urged the pope to use his visit to Czechoslovakia to "support striving after unity in truth and love."

Also in May 1990 the Czech National Assembly voted to permit private religious schools to function for the

124

first time in four decades. In addition, the education reform bill in Czechoslovakia incorporates seminary training
programs into the universities following patterns roughly
equivalent to those in existence at the end of World
War II. As welcome as such opportunities are for many,
they clearly are divisive as well.

On the other hand, the churches may be led to unite
as they face two massive issues that hang heavily over all
the region. One of these is the problem of air and water
pollution. The churches were among the first to give this
concern high visibility, addressing it as part of the World
Council of Churches call for action on "Justice, Peace and
the Integrity of Creation." The environmental problems of
Central and Eastern Europe are certain to become an urgently serious issue within the next few years. The second
massive issue could result from economic dislocation or
panic (see below, pp. 140–143). The transition to a market or mixed economy in the former Communist states
will impact every family. Nothing is so likely to under-
mine the confidence of people in their new governments
so quickly as lasting food shortages or long lines of people
seeking work. These region-wide issues may summon the
churches to ecumenical engagement.

Prophecy in Changed Circumstances

Those who were in the opposition movements in Poland,
Hungary and Czechoslovakia have had to discover both
the ambiguities of leadership and ways to continue their
prophetic stands from within the mainstream of society.
In some cases this is very difficult.

Christians in the former German Democratic Republic
have had the additional problem that their church now
must consider adopting the very different approach to
church-state relations that developed in the Federal Republic of Germany during the years since World War II.

East Berlin's Bishop Gottfried Forck has expressed concern that as the two Germanies become one nation, the church in the East is in danger of "losing our clarity" on the proper approach to the state. He described the "positive role as helpful critics" taken by the Federation of Evangelical Churches in the former GDR. He cited, as an example, how the church there took the position that "refusing to do military service is better than doing it."

Bishop Forck acknowledged in April 1990 that "such declarations would probably not be possible without repercussions in the Federal Republic because there are military officers in the FRG who say they are Christians. In the GDR, no officer belonged to the church."

The relation between church and state after the end of Communist domination in the GDR became very complex. Pastors and other church leaders were, at least temporarily, in positions of government responsibility. By the spring of 1990, the Mondays after Easter and Ascension Day became public holidays. Even under the Communists, however, the official holidays had included Good Friday, Easter Sunday, Pentecost Sunday and the Monday following, and two days at Christmas. Three other religious celebrations had been recognized as public holidays until 1967. They were the feast day of Corpus Christi, Reformation Day and Repentance Day. These issues are especially complex in an increasingly pluralistic nation.

Similar issues have been identified in Poland, Czechoslovakia and Romania. Although not as dramatically as in the former German Democratic Republic, religious leaders (lay and clergy) have been elected or appointed to official government positions in each of these countries. In the former GDR, for example, twenty-one pastors or theologians were elected to the parliament and the prime minister is a church official. Although there are good reasons why this happened, there are inherent problems as well. Some cite possible conflict of interest. Others believe that it is seldom wise for the church to prescribe a particular political solution. And still others raise the question whether the church abdicates its prophetic role once it, or its principal leaders, occupy seats of power.

Reconciliation and Forgiveness

Even though the revolutions in Central and Eastern Europe were nonviolent (except in the case of Romania), they were, nevertheless, revolutions. And (again, except in the case of Romania) there was an amazing readiness on the part of the new leaders to protect the dignity of those who were forced out of office and even a preparedness to forgive those who had been their oppressors.

In a message to the churches prepared on November 11, 1989, after the Wall had been opened, the president of the Federation of Evangelical Churches in the GDR urged Christians not to respond to their former oppressors with revenge. "We need to react humbly and without hostility," Bishop Werner Leich said.

On several occasions pastors intervened to protect members of the hated State Security Service, or Stasi. Church members also joined with members of the opposition group New Forum linking arms to prevent demonstrators from seeking retribution from party officials after their lavish lifestyles were revealed. The Rev. Werner Kraetschell told the BBC that "our people are in a very aggressive and angry mood. They feel they have been cheated for decades." Following a confrontation in Leipzig on December 18, the Rev. Günter Hanisch of the Nikolaikirche appealed for restraint during the weekly service.

In Poland and Hungary the electoral process created situations in which at least some of the former Communist leaders maintained a measure of responsibility. This was not the case in the former German Democratic Republic, however, where the most dramatic evidence of forgiveness was displayed. For a period the church there provided Erich and Margot Honecker with a place in which to live. After Honecker was forced to resign as party secretary he no longer had claim on his luxurious home located in an area of exclusive villas. The facility was, in fact, to be converted into a convalescent home. Facing charges for crimes against the state and suffering from incurable cancer, the seventy-seven-year-old Honecker requested admission to a Protestant home for the aged. East Berlin's United Church Bishop Gottfried Forck conditionally agreed, although he was concerned about the church's ability to provide protection.

Bishop Forck replied to the flurry of criticism that followed with an explanation that the church's teaching on forgiveness of sin and justification by grace applies to all persons, including Honecker and his wife.

The Honeckers were provided hospitality in the parsonage of a church-sponsored home in the town of Lobetal. The pastor who directs the home, Uwe Holmer, received two thousand letters and two bomb threats while the Honeckers were living there. He later explained that he had no sympathy for the old regime when he and his wife received the Honeckers into their parsonage as their personal guests. To the contrary, while Margot Honecker was the minister of education, the Holmer's had applied for admission to secondary schools for eight of their ten children. None was admitted, despite their good-to-excellent grades.

Nevertheless, Holmer said, "we carry no bitterness in our hearts because, as followers of Jesus, we have forgiven." He also cited the words of the founder of the Lobetal home, Friedrich von Bodelschwingh, who urged his co-workers to "turn no one away" and referred to the compassion of Jesus, who was concerned about the weary and heavy laden, as well as the homeless.

In a nine-point response to those who criticized the church's action, Holmer expressed his view that the issue was not concern for the Honeckers, but concern for the way "you and I, and our people" will make a transition to a democratic society in which the convictions of others are respected. After two months the Honeckers were moved to a Soviet military hospital near Potsdam where the former party secretary could also receive treatment for his terminal illness.

Another dramatic example of reconciliation took place in Prague eight days after a group of riot police had beaten and seriously wounded a group of students. The young men and women had demonstrated on the fiftieth anniversary of Nazi brutality against another group of students. During the demonstration, as a crowd of nearly eighty thousand began chanting, "We want peace and freedom, no more violence!" the riot police wounded 143 people in what had become known as the November 17th Massacre.

An American woman, Jana Kiely, whose parents had left Czechoslovakia in 1948, returned to her native land just before the Easter 1990 visit of Pope John Paul II. A friend described to her the dramatic rally on November 25, immediately following a celebration in the cathedral of the recent canonization of St. Agnes of Bohemia. The Civic Forum had called the rally on the Letna esplanade not far from the Cathedral and the Hradcany Castle. It was an emotional event. The moderator of the rally, Father Václav Malý, called Alexander Dubček forward. The one-time Communist official who had been deposed in 1968 held out his arms to the people and, referring to the canonization, said, "Now we are linked back with our history." The playwright Václav Havel spoke next: "We know what we want — truth, respect for human rights, freedom."

As Kiely, who is associate master of Harvard's Adams House, retells the story, the crowd was ecstatic. Father Malý knew he had his hands full as he faced nearly 250,000 persons. He knew that the people had demanded that the perpetrators of the massacre be apprehended.

Then the priest took an enormous risk. He called several police to the platform. "I have found a group of riot police who wish to apologize," he said. According to Kiely's friend, the crowd was tense and a menacing silence could be felt. "Will you accept their apology?" the priest asked, almost as though he was addressing his congregation at St. Gabriel's Church. Then, gradually, the crowd began to chant the words of the liturgy, *Od-pus-ti-me, od-pus-ti-me!* "We-for-give-you, we-for-give-you!" Father Malý then led the vast crowd in a recitation of the Lord's Prayer.

Kiely's friend told her, "It was the first time that we knew we were all one. We knew that if only the Communists would leave us alone we would be all right." That reconciling moment was a turning point, a kind of resurrection for the people of Czechoslovakia. It was an eloquent statement that emphasized the nonviolent and essentially religious character of what came to be called the Velvet Revolution. It also provided a declaration of the willingness of the people to seek reconciliation.

On the other hand, the summary execution of Romania's President Nicolae Ceausescu revealed how explosive forty years of bottled-up anger can be. One of the great fears that haunts thousands of Central and Eastern Europeans is that this anger will remain with people whose patience has real limits. They hope that the anger can be dissipated and that sufficient political and economic progress will be made that the people will retain their sense of accomplishment and pride. The churches will surely monitor the situation and seek to encourage positive steps so that bloodshed can be avoided.

CHAPTER ELEVEN

Storm Clouds

Their Undigested History

Suddenly, the people of Central and Eastern Europe have discovered that they need to take responsibility for their own futures. In the period when Communists were in power, their lives — like the economy — were planned. Many now are discovering that their past could come back to haunt them. Without the controls enforced by the often oppressive regimes there is a real danger that the new freedoms could provide a license for warring nationalism and resurgent anti-Semitism.

Wolfgang Steckel, the pastor of the Petruskirche in Dessau, wrote to the other partner churches right after the Berlin Wall was pierced. "We Germans have not quite digested our history between 1914 and 1945," he acknowledged. "We allowed ourselves to be integrated into the two power blocs. Now our history is catching up with us. The mistrust of our neighbor states proves it. Hundreds of thousands of our East German citizens swarm over West Germany like locusts. The urge to recoup on something denied in the past is very strong. Stronger nationalistic [attitudes] may emerge here. Our hostility toward Poles and the guest workers from China, Vietnam, Angola and Mozambique only point up that danger."

Intolerance toward foreign workers has been increasingly evident. The Rev. Almuth Berger, who was appointed by the new government to work with nationals of other countries employed in what had been the GDR, believes that one factor in the prejudice and economic bias being expressed toward foreigners is the background of the people in National Socialism (Nazism), which, she points out, "has never been reappraised in the GDR." According to the East Berlin pastor, "Much which had been swept under the carpet now is coming to light again." Another factor in the prejudice, she says, was an atmosphere of intolerance that prevailed under the Communist Party — an atmosphere that denied the value of other opinions and other ways of life.

During the winter of 1990, East Germany's interim prime minister Hans Modrow expressed concern that a neo-Nazi party, the right-wing Republican Party, was attempting to gain a foothold in the former GDR as it had in the Federal Republic. The Republican Party, which is headed by a man who had been one of Hitler's SS troops, received up to 20 percent of the votes in some working-class districts of West Berlin. Modrow's concern, expressed in a letter to a Los Angeles rabbi who had asked whether a united Germany would take steps to educate citizens about the Holocaust and to provide legal sanctions against anti-Semitism and other forms of bigotry, was probably a propaganda ploy to gain support in the elections that followed. Mr. Modrow cited how artists and writers in East Germany had dealt with the Holocaust; neither he nor the West German Chancellor Helmut Kohl promised to take steps to incorporate the subject in school curricula.

A different problem faces the Roman Catholic majority in Hungary. There, for generations, the church's ties to the nation's leaders alienated many people. In feudal times the church became a large landowner and it exerted substantial political and economic power through the Habsburg era. When the Communists came to power many priests, monks and nuns, whose orders had been legally dissolved, gathered informal community groups to continue religious education, youth ministries and a semi-underground Christian fellowship. These groups were subjected to frequent police attacks, even after the government in 1977 signed the Helsinki agreements on human rights. A particular target was the Bulanyist movement, whose members were principled in their refusal to serve in the military. The Catholic hierarchy sided with the government, disciplining the priests who sometimes continued their priestly functions without direct ties to their bishops.

In the new situation, where the government has promised an option of an alternative to military service, the church hierarchy is struggling to find a new identity. Some church members wonder how it will address the major social problems of alcoholism, suicide and divorce and how it will reclaim the loyalties of the informal Christian fellowships that developed in the period of oppression. The new Roman Catholic identity in Hungary may be built in part on its present ecumenical ties to Protestant communities, especially to the Reformed Church in Hungary. In any case it clearly will need to deal with issues from its history, some of which are awkward and embarrassing.

Beneath the surface throughout the reign lies an awareness that within the national psyches of many of the countries there is latent anti-Semitism which in the past too often was fanned into violence by appeals to nationalism. The churches, embarrassed over their silence during the time of Hitler, recognize this tendency in ways that others do not yet acknowledge. Perhaps it is that liturgically, at least, the churches affirm the need for confession and the potential for redemption. Each nation has its own manifestations of prejudice and hatred just as each has its own history. Yet, all the nations of Central and Eastern Europe share anguished, though sometimes silent, memories of the Holocaust. As they celebrate the changes that already have taken place in one country after another, the church leaders also have begun to work on the need to change attitudes and personal reactions. They are realistic as they recognize that psychological walls and traditional animosities will take a long time to overcome.

Although Gunnar Staalsett, the general secretary of the Lutheran World Federation, welcomes the reaffirmation of cultural traditions and national identities that are sweeping the region, he also warns that these developments could lead to a "resurgence of a new nationalism and a demonic allegiance to the gods of blood and soil and race." Staalsett is concerned that old ethnic and religious prejudices could lead the churches into becoming "uncritical handmaids of new national ideologies."

Two leading German bishops, however, believe that there is no reason to fear nationalist tendencies as the people of East and West Germany move toward unity. Christoph Demke of Magdeburg in the former GDR and Martin Kruse of West Berlin agreed that nationalism is not a factor but the "feeling that we belong together" is. Kruse said that German unity is "a gift of God." He also said that "Germans must accept themselves and their place in history." He indicated that he could not understand why "anyone should be afraid of this."

The hope that Gunnar Staalsett sees is that in recent decades Eastern and Central Europeans have begun to understand the collective nature of society, expressed as a sense of "solidarity." Ironically, he believes this has been a legacy of Marxist doctrine as it was tested against biblical and ethical standards. Christians and others from around the world carried on an almost constant dialogue on the impact on the churches of secular Marxism. These conversations took place under the auspices of the World Council of Churches, the Conference of European Churches and in various confessional settings.

During a 1990 visit to the United States, in which he spoke at a two-day Washington symposium on pol-

itics and ethics, Dr. Staalsett explained that he believes
that "if there is anything that the churches in all countries have to contribute to the new situation in Europe it
is an understanding of human dignity, rights and values
that brings together the two traditions of the individual
and the collective good." The churches will have numerous opportunities as the new Germany takes shape within
a new Europe.

Minority Churches Face Special Problems

The atmosphere of intolerance has very deep roots
throughout Europe. The Nazi party of Adolf Hitler built
its doctrine of Aryan superiority on assumptions of dis-
respect and hatred that in turn were based on historic
animosities. Many of these assumptions and animosities
continue today, only slightly below the surface with religious as well as ethnic expressions. These may have
particular impact on minority churches.

Protestants in Poland, for example, increasingly are
concerned that, perhaps unintentionally, the dominant
Roman Catholic population will limit the religious opportunities available to non-Catholics. Tension between
Protestants and Catholics is real. There have been reports, for example, that unused and underused Lutheran
church buildings have been taken over by Roman Catholics. Barbara Engholc-Narzynska, who heads the Polish
Bible Society, says that Protestants in Poland find life
harder now than under Communist rule partly because the
supervision of the churches by the state has now been dis-
continued. She recognizes that "our problems began under
the old system and the new government has inherited
them."

According to Piotr Dajludzionek of the Baptist Union
of Poland, the problem is especially acute in small villages. Nonetheless, he says that in many areas, especially in

urban centers, relations between Roman Catholic leaders and evangelical pastors remain excellent. Difficult circumstances have been reported in Hungary, where János Viczián, president of the Baptist Union there, reported that one priest blocked a Baptist crusade in a small town and another refused to let a Pentecostal pastor lead devotions in a Budapest hospital chapel.

In May 1990, the Polish government minister for church affairs assured Bishop Herbert W. Chilstrom of the Evangelical Lutheran Church in America that the Polish government "stands firm in the conviction that the country should not be dominated by any one denomination." Nevertheless, the Polish Ecumenical Council sent a message to Prime Minister Tadeusz Mazowiecki at about the same time warning that the religious instruction soon to begin in Polish schools will "be a breach of basic equality." Such instruction is expected to be mandatory as a result of requests from the Roman Catholic Church, which urged compulsory religious training in state-run schools despite the objections of nonbelievers and minority Christian groups. The Ecumenical Council argues that such training should take place within the churches and should be on a voluntary basis in both the state schools and church classrooms. The Ecumenical Council also asked that Lutheran children be provided with a Lutheran instructor just as Catholic youngsters will learn from a Roman Catholic teacher. The Ecumenical Council asked that a commission to be established to work on these and other related issues.

In countries like Romania where Orthodoxy is traditionally strong, members of free churches, like the Baptists, are especially concerned over potential conflict with Eastern Orthodox leaders. Cornel Fedor, a Baptist from Comanesti, Romania, reports that Orthodox priests are claiming that "Baptists are stealing their members." In an increasingly tense situation in Romania, Orthodox leaders look upon Baptists as a sect while the Baptists say

that the Orthodox hierarchy was too close to the Ceausescu government. The Romanian government's former
minister of religion, Nicolae Stoicescu, confirmed these
suspicions with a public acknowledgment that the Romanian Orthodox Church was under the "direct control and
supervision" of Ceausescu's secret police. Nevertheless,
Stoicescu favored a close relation between the Orthodox
and the state in the future because, he said, "the church
[of which the Orthodox is dominant] has a major role
to play in rehabilitating the Romanian spirit." Anxieties
are reflected as minority churches ask how the "Romanian spirit" is defined. Circumstances like these make
continued ecumenical conversations especially important
in countries where there are dominant religious groups
and minority churches. Such circumstances also call for
any infringement of religious liberty to be monitored.

German Unification

Probably no question in Central and Eastern Europe will
have a more widespread impact than the unification of
Germany. The question poses issues that reach far beyond the borders of the two Germanies: those who recall
the economic and military power of the Third Reich
are anxious and cautiously scan the political horizons for
some indication of what unification will mean to them.
This concern lingers even after the signing in November 1990 of a German-Polish treaty acknowledging their
common border. In addition, the question summons concerns because those in the European Community are at
the threshold of broader economic unity. How will their
dreams for a peacefully united Europe be affected by the
involvement of the former German Democratic Republic,
impoverished as it is? And the question poses, also, the
problem of relations to other parts of the world, including the poor nations of the southern hemisphere. All these

issues may puzzle the politicians who must balance their own visions with electoral realities. Church leaders bring two additional factors to their views of the question of unification: They bring ecumenical experience, in which dialogue with colleagues from other nations is valued and affirmed. And they bring a recognition that the common good, as well as self-interest, needs to be considered.

There also are special problems for the churches inherent in plans for national unification. The churches developed separate patterns in East and West despite their common histories and the communication links described in chapter 1. The differences can be seen most acutely in relation to the "church tax" levied in the Federal Republic and in the religious education available in the public schools there. In addition, German Christians are well aware of the fears of their neighbors, especially in Poland, concerning the potential strength of a unified nation on their western borders. The leaders of the Federation of Protestant Churches in the former GDR and of the Evangelical Church in Germany sought to deal with these issues in a joint declaration released on January 17, 1990.

In their statement, the bishops and representatives of the two churches expressed "gratitude and joy" about the changes that had taken place in the GDR and especially for the success of the nonviolent demonstrations. Noting the role of the churches in the events of the fall and winter of 1989, the two groups affirmed that they had "experienced anew...the political impact of the spiritual commission of the church of Jesus Christ." Specifically, they cited the political effect of the commitment written into the constitutions of both churches to the "special communion of the entire Protestant Christendom in Germany." This, they said, has been practiced "in countless relationships." The leaders announced that they had agreed to set up a commission to guide the reunion of the churches. They also addressed the need to "take seriously the concerns and reservations of our friends in

other countries and our European neighbors against German unification." They announced their intent "to court
the trust" of these friends and urged "clarity in present-
ing German intentions and caution in implementing new
unity" as ways to encourage trust both at home and
abroad.

There is also concern that reunification will lead toward
what Bishop Johannes Hempel describes as "materialistic
temptations." The contrast between the economies of East
and West and between the standards of living in the two
areas could hardly be greater. Hempel believes that the
churches must continue to encourage simplicity as well as
to remind political leaders of the needs of disadvantaged
persons, including the elderly, the handicapped, children
and women. "True life in the fullness of Christ is not to
be confused with material abundance," he has counseled
church members in both East and West.

Another area of conflict involves the different theological and ethical attitudes toward abortion that developed
in East and West Germany since the end of World War II.
Both Roman Catholic and Protestant bishops in West Germany have condemned the freedom of choice abortion law
in the former German Democratic Republic as well as the
political compromise not to change that law for two years
following unification. The "basis of union" document approved by leaders of the two Germanies provided that
after two years the new legislature would consider laws
regarding abortion for the united Germany. The Protestant bishop of West Berlin, Martin Kruse, and the Catholic
bishop of Mainz, Karl Lehmann, issued a joint statement
declaring the East German law permitting an abortion during the first twelve weeks of pregnancy "irreconcilable with
fundamental convictions of the Christian faith and the
church." In the Federal Republic of Germany a woman
seeking an abortion needs to obtain a legal "exception"
that could be granted only if the birth of a child would
create a hardship in her life. Such exceptions are rou-

tinely granted, except in Bavaria, which is overwhelmingly Roman Catholic.

While celebrating the fact that the German people and their churches can now be reunited, Christians there and around the world are conscious of the fact that unification is not without its problems. Ecumenical leaders, especially, are concerned that as Germany is reborn it will see itself within the context of the whole community of European nations.

CHAPTER TWELVE

Building New Societies

Economic Factors

Christians in Central and Eastern European nations are worried about the economic impact of the rapid changes that took place in 1989 and early 1990. They are concerned about the futures of their religious institutions; they are even more worried about how their nations, and the peoples of their nations, will move into the very different world of a market-driven economy. In some cases, at least, Christians are seeking ways to make a prophetic witness in their societies as they look at economic issues.

The East German pastor whose ties to Czechoslovakia and to Great Britain, West Germany and the United States have been so important for his congregation in Dessau (and for churches in the other four nations) puts it this way: When "unification of East and West Germany occurs, we should establish an economy which will not suffocate weaker neighboring peoples. But how," asks Wolfgang Steckel, "is this to be done? Isn't the strong one always the victor in the competition within a free market economy? . . . Only when we attempt to understand one another can the walls of fear and mistrust come down, and controversies be reconciled."

One summary of such pleas for sensitive understanding

was offered by the Rev. Paul F. Wilson, who reported on a meeting early in 1990 of the Churches' Human Rights Program. Wilson, a staff member of the Christian Church (Disciples of Christ), said that Central and Eastern European Christians fear that the events of 1989 will be misunderstood in the United States as "a great victory of capitalism over socialism." People with whom he spoke at the human rights meeting explain the breaching of the Iron Curtain not as "a repudiation of socialism as an economic system" but as "a repudiation of totalitarianism as a political system." Many persons in Poland, Hungary, Czechoslovakia and the former German Democratic Republic favor a mixed economy rather than the imposition of capitalism in the form of a pure market economy.

Christians in Eastern and Central Europe, according to Wilson, are extremely concerned that "tremendous pressures" on new governments to deliver formerly unavailable basic goods to people who "want it now" may create conditions for a new kind of economic tyranny. He heard that the chief complaint in some parts of the former German Democratic Republic was the unavailability of cut flowers, an important commodity and a symbol of hope to a desperate people. An expressed fear in Europe was that if the two Germanies were brought together too quickly "East Germany could become a kind of Third World supplier to West Germany."

Wilson also heard Eastern and Central European participants in the human rights meeting express anxiety that new problems — bureaucratic, financial and economic — could seriously threaten the accomplishments of the 1989 nonviolent revolution.

In his visit to Czechoslovakia in April 1990, Pope John Paul II warned that getting rid of Communism is not enough if it simply means replacing it with the "secularism, indifference, hedonistic consumerism, practical materialism and also the formal atheism" that "plague the West." His concern was illustrated by Milan Opočensky, the Czech theologian who now heads the World Alliance of Reformed Churches. Opočensky described the new temptations of the people in his country. "They rush to catch up with the developed countries. They join the hunt for profit." One result, he believes, is that "concern for public affairs is already diminishing" since what he called the "revolution of lights and candles." He observed that one result of the new economic possibilities is that "personal responsibility is lessening."

In this Opočensky shares the concern of other theologians in the region that "it would be tragic if the present positive changes mean more poverty and suffering in other parts of the world. Eastern Europe must not become an ally in the undeclared war against the poor."

A theology professor from Jena, Klaus-Peter Hertzsch, has warned against a future "rule by millionaires" that would replace the rule of Communist officials. Hertzsch believes that the people who had rid themselves of so many fetters and chains are in danger of being shackled by chain stores. He warned against what he called the "merry-go-round" of stress and consumerism, of life that comes to nothing. He urged the people of the former GDR, as they strive after prosperity, not to forget the real poverty in the Third World.

The general secretary of the Lutheran World Federation, Gunnar Staalsett, also reflects the concerns of many Lutherans from East and Central Europe. "Replacing the failed ideologies of Marxist socialism with morally flawed materialism and greed could mean that if 'capitalism' triumphs, the effect on the churches in the East could be as damaging as it has been on the churches of the West," he says. Even Aleksandr Solzhenitsyn has indicated that given the choice between the external evil of Soviet communism and the internal, seductive evil of Western materialism, he would not willingly choose the latter.

The potential impact of the changed economic situation on the churches themselves already is creating tensions, especially in relation to the unification of Germany. In West Germany, the churches have become dependent on the so-called church tax, collected by the state from all citizens unless they specifically request exemption. While acknowledging that the West German churches made generous and "life-saving" contributions to East German churches and other international causes, church officials in the former GDR saw values in the system of voluntary contributions that they had learned to live with since 1952. Still, economic changes in East Germany will almost certainly increase costs beyond what the churches can afford. Subsidies on goods will be cut, prices will rise, and churches may not be able to keep salaries in line with the increased cost of living.

Educational Opportunities

Throughout Central and Eastern Europe the educational question is urgent because the schools run by the former Communist governments have been so thoroughly discredited and because the churches are at present ill-prepared to fill the vacuum. They had, since the beginning of World War II, only minimal opportunities to exercise educational ministries. Sometimes their contact with young people was strictly forbidden. Today they lack personnel, resources and experience to offer organized youth activities or educational programs on a broad scale.

Dr. Josef Hromádka, a pastor of the Evangelical Church of Czech Brethren and part of the new government, reports that "there are so many young people now coming to the churches and putting the question, 'Please tell us what Christianity is all about.'" He observes that "this is a new chance for the churches — but it is a very demanding one." In Czechoslovakia and elsewhere in the region young people come to the churches partly because now they are free to do so and also because the churches have caught their attention and won their respect.

Stressing what he called a religious revival in Central and Eastern Europe, Pope John Paul II has invited the young people of the former Communist countries to meet with him during the Sixth World Youth Day scheduled to be held in August 1991 at the Shrine of the black Madonna in Czestochowa, Poland. The pope referred to the Youth Day as "a pilgrimage of freedom across the frontiers of states which, more and more, are opening to Christ, redeemer of humanity."

On the other hand, the Rev. Rudi Panke, who directs youth work for the Federation of Evangelical Churches, sees what he describes as a crisis among young people in the former German Democratic Republic. He said that the mass exodus of youth to West Germany was due to the "spiritual and moral fragmentation" that resulted from the Communists' "ill-conceived concept of society and [the party's] unrealistic image of humanity." Some of the youth left because of lack of trust, according to Panke, while others "felt insecure, resigned, or went over to the extreme right or left."

Educational reforms in the former GDR are being pressed by churches and individuals who were consistently critical of the educational policies of Margot Honecker. For a quarter of a century Honecker had headed the school system for her husband's government. Not only are party politics being eliminated from the classrooms but educators are seeking ways to bring back "a sense of awe and wonder" through attention to poetry and theology. In the Heiligenstadt district, a Christian believer by the name of Walter Henning was named superintendent of schools almost immediately after the Honecker government fell. Henning had previously been denied a position in the schools. Not only did the new superintendent remove three principals who he believed supported Margot Honecker's policies, but Henning also wrote a new civics textbook to replace materials that taught Marxist doctrine.

Even relatively simple issues became problems. Wolfgang Steckel has described how the teachers and parents of the Dessau school district now have to replace a curriculum that "is broken down." He asks, "What should now be taught? That is a difficult task for the teachers. They are not accustomed to decide for themselves. Previously they were told what to say — nearly word for word." This, too, becomes an issue for the churches, which have at least a little more experience in the planning and execution of meetings and programs. So Steckel called the teachers and parents together. "In former times it was unthinkable for a minister to invite teachers to a meeting. There was not only the Wall between East and West, but many questions, relations and facts were taboo. . . . Freedom," he says, "includes a great excitement — but anxiety, too, because we have no experience."

Other East German pastors are being invited to participate in events at universities and teacher-training schools. Whereas public school teachers were among the most ideologically regimented groups, at present the schools are looking to the churches for assistance in reworking their curriculum and educational system. Educators in Potsdam want to develop several school programs that would serve children with different abilities. They want to return to educational traditions that first were eliminated by the Nazis who, like the Communists, insisted on an ideologically based curriculum.

In the Berlin-Brandenburg area of the former GDR, there has been a slow but steady increase in the number of children registered for Christian education provided outside the schools by members of Lutheran, Reformed or United congregations. Until 1989, parents in certain professions, including teaching, could not enroll their children in such programs. The end of that taboo may account for the gradual increase in registration, though the provost of the Berlin-Brandenburg churches, Hans Otto Furian, says "there is no longer any doubt that church people [in this region] will press for religious instruction within the schools."

Protestant churches in the former GDR now are demanding the right to teach religion in the state-supported schools. Bishop Christoph Demke of Magdeburg wants the new constitution to guarantee the right to teach religion in the schools. At the same time, he acknowledges that instructors will need to be trained because the present teachers "know so little about religion and the history of the church."

Another East German bishop, Werner Leich of Thuringia, has indicated that although "financial independence from the state and a separate program of Christian education" were important when the church was challenging the government's claim to a monopoly in education and leadership, people now recognize that "German history, literature and culture cannot be taught without a basic knowledge of the tenets of the Christian faith."

External Religious Organizations

Churches in several countries of Central and Eastern Europe have expressed concern about a deluge of well-meaning but overwhelming support being furnished by some Western religious organizations. The ecumenical council in the former GDR warned against the "mass of Christian initiatives from hundreds of Western church sources [that are] currently flooding Eastern Europe."

As soon as the borders were opened, many relief programs moved in and groups were eager to distribute Bibles and religious literature. Others began beaming fundamentalist radio programs from transmitters in neighboring countries. In many cases the offers of help were as welcome as they were generous. Individual Christians and their churches had urgent need for food and other relief supplies. In some instances the churches became the distribution points for foodstuffs, medicines and other material aid that was provided to any person in need. In several countries, Bibles and books for religious instruction had been virtually unavailable for decades, so the need for publications was equally great. The United Bible Societies, of which the American Bible Society is a member, has undertaken a massive effort to supply large numbers of Bibles throughout Central and Eastern Europe.

In certain cases, however, the support was tied to political or religiously divisive views. Reports of confusion, frustration and desperation began to circulate by early spring 1990. The former Romanian minister of religious affairs, Professor Nicolae Stoicescu, described as "a serious problem" the influx of evangelical missionary groups that he called "neo-Protestantism." He indicated that many of these are from the United States and that "they are difficult to engage in dialogue." Among groups that have confused the religious landscape in Central and Eastern Europe are Eastern "gurus," New Age movements and Mormons, each claiming to represent certainty or Truth. At least one Baptist fellowship in Central and Eastern Europe found itself caught in a dispute whose origins were among congregations in United States. Understandably the church leaders of such countries as Hungary, Czechoslovakia, Romania and the former German Democratic Republic prefer to have aid channeled through ecumenical organizations with which they long have had contacts of mutuality and partnership.

Need for Renewed Confidence and Trust

The united Germany is only one nation in which confidence and trust among the peoples needs to be renewed. A widespread and serious issue is the result of an unwilling-

148

ness to cooperate and a lack of mutual respect among the
ethnic groups that make up the populations of such nations as Czechoslovakia and Romania. These attitudes are
present in other areas as well. Generally the churches, or
more precisely the church leaders in each country, recognize this need. Both the World Council of Churches and
the Conference of European Churches have raised these
issues with the national church officials. The Lutheran
World Federation and the World Alliance of Reformed
Churches also have pointed to these problems.

A specific area in which confidence and trust must be
restored relates to the roles that some Christians and some
church leaders played in relation to the former regimes. In
Romania, for example, the Ceausescu regime found ways
to infiltrate all segments of society — even the church.
Government informers and the secret police were everywhere. Because their activities and former roles were so
greatly feared and because suspicion was virtually universal, the new society will be weakened until confidence
and trust are restored. Recrimination toward even minor
collaborators will delay that sense of national unity and
direction that is so essential to the development of democratic structures. Furthermore, many individuals from the
Ceausescu government, including members of the dreaded
Securitate, are among key figures in the National Salvation
Front. Since the churches, as well as other institutions,
were permeated by informers and collaborators, they will
not find it easy to provide the leadership needed to sur-
mount the skepticism and distrust that is so widespread.

Need for Clarity of Purpose

New occasions teach new duties and changed circumstances create different problems. Particularly after the
excitement and euphoria of the events of 1989, the let-
down in morale and confusion over purpose and direction

were to be expected. The churches of Central and Eastern Europe, which helped to provide perspective all during the years of authoritarian rule and a sense of direction as the regimes were falling apart, now have a new task.

During the spring of 1990, Wolfgang Steckel of Dessau described the situation as he saw it: "We have lost the great expectations of last autumn. That is natural. At this time we are unable to form an idea of the future. We demanded democracy," he wrote to friends in the West, "we demanded freedom and permission to travel, without an exact idea about the reality of our demands. Now the reality overtakes us and we are aware that democracy and freedom mean conflict, compromise and renunciation. All that is new for us. In the last forty years we assumed that if the hated government is passed over all circumstances automatically will be better. But that is an illusion and we are a bit disappointed. That is our situation. We are glad to be free from the pressure of the government, but we are a bit anxious as we look forward."

One of the seven presidents of the World Council of Churches is Bishop Johannes Hempel from what had been the German Democratic Republic. He believes that the churches in the region now must "help see that illusions are replaced by a realistic hope." He told the World Council's Central Committee in March 1990 that the churches in countries where Communist rule has been replaced will need to help their societies draw the difficult lines between justice and revenge and between a "legitimate pride in a nation and a pompous, ritualistic nationalism." The Lutheran bishop further said that to provide such leadership it will need "to recognize its own share in guilt for the past" and to find ways to continue to work with grassroots movements. Speaking specifically of the challenge that East German Christians now face, Hempel said that the church must keep a global and ecumenical perspective. "East Germany is not Germany," he said, and "Germany is not Europe, and Europe is not the world."

Although at the moment there may be more confusion than clarity of purpose, it seems reasonable to believe that the Christian community that had steadfastly held to its purposes and which provided stimulation, direction and leadership to the democracy movement will help the new Central and Eastern Europe clarify its goals and objectives. It will do this out of its own life. The clarity will come from the diaconal ministries of the churches as they seek to serve others. It will come from the women and men who refused to compromise their integrity and who, with considerable risk, found ways to continue in dialogue with despotic leaders. It will come from the ecumenical search for justice and peace and the integrity of the environment. It will come as the church opens itself to listen to the cries and appeals of working people and of youth. And it will come as the church risks speaking for those in the society whose voices are ignored.

Justice Comes and Will Come

As he had on so many previous occasions, on the Sunday after the Wall was pierced, Pastor Helmut turned to the Bible. The people of Martin Luther's *Stadtkirche* in Wittenberg were accustomed to the way their pastor opened the scriptures to them as together they discovered how the ancient texts spoke to contemporary events. Like most other clergy Pastor Helmut used the lectionary passage in Luke 18. Jesus' parable of the importunate widow also is the story of a "judge who neither feared God nor had respect for people." Filled with determination, the widow kept coming to him until the judge granted her justice, but only because she kept bothering him.

In the parable Jesus sought to encourage the people not to lose heart. "Will not God grant justice to his chosen ones who cry to him day and night? Will he delay long in helping them? I tell you, he will quickly grant justice to them."

On that Sunday in 1989 it must have been particularly exciting to hear that passage read. Nevertheless, the promise of the parable stretches into the future for the people of Central and Eastern Europe. More than we may realize, the promise of the parable presses our futures as well.

Westerners may read these reports with a mixture of excitement and amazement, with heightened expectations and with earnest prayers that what has happened in Europe in the months since the beginning of 1989 will survive anxious, troublous times. Perhaps the courage and faithfulness of Christians and others in Poland, Hungary, Czechoslovakia and East Germany may even inspire peaceful achievements elsewhere. There is a direct challenge to North American Christians in the words of Milan Opočensky, who told a group of Princeton Theological Seminary alumni/ae that they share with European churches "the most important task to be a prophetic voice, to keep the humanity of the entire world in the forefront of concern."

Our hopes, and fears, have been expressed well by Paul E. Starr of Princeton University: "The world's new realities are our renewed possibilities. But to realize those possibilities will require imagination, a sense of history and hard thought."

That is also the challenge facing the churches of Central and Eastern Europe. Theologically, many of those who worked so hard and risked so much in 1989 would say that, along with a tested faith and strong ecumenical ties, the churches need to bring "imagination, a sense of history and hard thought" to the Europe that is emerging. It is a challenge that many American Christians will gladly share.

Personal Postscript from (East) Germany

I like to think of myself as an ecumenical Christian, a world citizen. I find myself driven to international — even global — interests. I also look upon myself as a journalist, trained in the arts of interviewing and listening as well as of writing, committed to help my readers see beyond particular events to the meanings of those events, and pledged not only to accuracy but to telling a story fairly through the lives and words of others.

In one sense, that paragraph describes why I undertook to write this book. As change swept across Central and Eastern Europe, I became convinced that the Holy Spirit was at work and that church history was taking place, even though most observers perceived the events as essentially social, political and economic. This volume details my conviction.

At this point I need also to acknowledge that I am an American, writing mainly for an American audience. Though my faith has provided me with an intercultural family and a global identity, I see the world through the admittedly parochial eyes of an American, a Protestant and a white male. Even if I wanted to, I could not escape those facts. It is especially important in this book for me to confess that I am an American. I use the verb "confess" in the same way that I speak of confessing (that is, affirming) my faith and of confessing (that is, admitting) my sin. I am an American and

I observed the changes in Central and Eastern Europe as an American. I cannot be completely objective. And I certainly cannot adequately describe how those months felt to the people who experienced them.

It is therefore important for me, and for the reader, that this book end with a postscript written by a person who lived through these extraordinary events and who today lives in one of the changed societies. Christa Göbel is an ecumenical person with a global perspective, as I am. But not only has she seen the dramatic events and heard the stories first-hand, she is a product of a society that changed. She felt the joy and the pain of that change.

Christa writes out of her own experience in what was the German Democratic Republic. She makes no claim to speak about other countries or even to speak for other East Germans. Nevertheless, her testimony is authentic. I read her postscript as an important corrective to what I have written, for she brings a perspective that could come only from inside the change. I am grateful to her.

J. MARTIN BAILEY

I have listened to the author. And the reaction I offer is *one* of the possible reactions of the people concerned, namely my own.

I am Christa Göbel, a forty-six-year-old pastor of the Pomeranian Evangelical Church in the former German Democratic Republic (working in ecumenism and the training of Christian educators). I was born in Berlin in 1944, a baby of those nights of bombing, and grew up as a post-war child in the Eastern sector of a divided Berlin (with a few years of schooling in West Berlin). In East Berlin I also experienced the day when the wall was built and many of the following years with the wall — my studies, ordination and first parish. In 1975 I moved to Greifswald, where I am still living today.

The way of our church in our society was to some extent my own: Western ties, loyalty to the faith expressed in opposition, cautious rethinking, attempts at dialogue, assistance to people and critical solidarity (and sometimes a mixture of all that!).

The "door in the wall" at Berlin-Friedrichstrasse opened again for me after twenty years in 1981 for an official journey on behalf of the church. A great privilege — and so difficult to integrate into everyday life! The experience was repeated: new friends, joy, temptations and, each time, a homecoming. Despite all my criticism of the internal situation I felt I was a citizen of the German Democratic Republic, especially when I came up against arrogance or ignorance on the "other side."

In September 1989 I paid my first visit to the U.S.A. There I certainly met some like-minded people. But there were some to whom I had first to explain that in addition to "Germany" there was also a "German Democratic Republic," or why I did not think it better to remain in Chicago and why I was not happy about the GDR refugees pouring over the open Hungarian/Austrian border. Paths to freedom? Were we simply too cowardly — or had we failed? Was our church appeal "to stay where God had put us" really pastoral support for free consent or a legalism of the ghetto that no longer convinced anyone? We "established" people had often exhorted the groups and young people in our congregations to be cautious and patient, indeed to be diplomatic. Was this really a contribution to peace or simply to stabilizing the system?

Despite a number of indications the turning point finally took us by surprise. As late as in June 1989 Erich Honecker came to Greifswald cathedral and attended his first (and last) service of worship during his period in office. On October 18 the same year, the day he resigned, our first large gathering to pray for peace was held in the same place, followed by a demonstration. The period of change had started for us as well.

Special highlights in the process for me were the possibility to touch the Berlin wall and being allowed to stand

and dance on it and wave; and also my membership in
the New Forum and the good unexpected opportunities
for cooperation with the schools; but above all, time and
again, the prayers for peace with the many expectant eyes
in front of us and all around us.

In this study I have recognized many familiar things as
in a mirror. So I must say to the author, "Yes, that is what
it was like, and it is good that you have described it so
sensitively and tried to see what we can all learn from it."
But I must also ask, "Why are the colors used sometimes
so deceptively clear?" It seems as if from 1945 to 1989 we
lived exclusively in "suffering and pain," "totalitarianism,
oppression and persecution." The church alone (and especially its leaders!) brought a few spots of color into the
somber picture by "faith, witness, heroic pastors and even
dialogue." My own experience of these (almost all) years
of my life was more ambivalent and diverse: indeed there
was light and darkness, constraint and freedom, faith and
unbelief, pain and joy. And in and through all of this we
experienced God's sustaining strength even in those days.
But not because of our merits.

As a church we certainly also shared in the ambivalence
of the situation. We endeavored to serve Christ in human
beings but were tied up at the same time in structures
of collaboration with oppression. We tried to provide free
spaces for many people but at the same time our belief
in real change was much too faltering. It would certainly
not be appropriate to portray us as "saints." Nor were
the changes made by the candles that we carried from
the altars into the streets. The time was ripe according
to the will of God (and as a consequence of changes in
the USSR) and so we were simply able to cooperate with
him, sometimes without yet really understanding what was
happening.

And now in 1991? What can we do in cooperation
with God today? The feeling of exhilaration seems to
have petered out. Were we not strong enough? Would

we really have had an opportunity of trying to find a "third approach" between socialism and capitalism? Economic constraints, human yearnings, historical roots and diplomatic skill have tipped the scales. Now we are part of the German Federal Republic with its hard currency and valuable passport, its economic structures and the freedom proclaimed in its constitution, with its philosophy of affluence and its (Gulf war) taxes. And at the same time we are the second-class East, with an ailing past and present, where so much is now falling apart — juridically, economically, morally and psychologically. This tension is hard to bear. Some have found satisfaction in their own business, a period of study abroad or some new political or social commitment. Many others have found themselves unemployed, devalued, out on the street without prospects, and are looking for a scapegoat, e.g., in foreigners. Most of us are facing great insecurity in almost every realm of life. Little has been done to come to terms with the past.

And what about the church? For many it has become the "black" successor to the former "red" authorities. (Many former staff of our regional church now occupy political posts.) But often people expect the church to help when the social net breaks or in the search for a new ethical approach. There is so much we could do now: is it right for us to do it all? Are we able to? I have now become much more patient with my Western colleagues in the ministry because I am learning how difficult it is really to be the Church when you enjoy social recognition. We are still trying to find our way.

The reunification of the church is also a painful process. We in the East have lived off money from the church in the West for a long time, sometimes taking this too much for granted, and this is still the case. But does this mean it is right to adopt Western church practices, such as forms of training, church taxes, religious education in schools and military chaplaincy, at breakneck speed? And even if it is right, should these not be implemented in a new way?

Where is the "third way" here between the church in a social ghetto and the socially dependent church? Many West
German Christians are disappointed by our "rapid surren-
der." How can the experience gained in our own church
history bear fruit today? There too we are still searching —
sometimes just for the next step. Yes, "at the moment"
there is "more confusion than clarity of purpose" (p. 150).

Nevertheless, what confidence the author of this study
still has in the socially creative power of our faith (cf.
pp. 150–151! I find this almost intimidating and at least
amazing. Is it childish or eschatological faith — or both?
I personally often still sense bereavement on taking leave
of so much that constituted life, and fear in the midst
of so much uncertainty which threatens to outweigh the
gratitude, as well as a tremendous burden of responsibility.

But then I also feel courage, indeed confidence. After
all:

• We experienced God's lasting strength for decades. That
  will prevail.

• The special experience of our fall revolution may teach us
  hope, above all. God can really open up new ways now as
  well.

• Our tasks increase daily whenever the needs of human beings — also worldwide — set the church's agenda. So we
  are needed.

• There are many at our side: Christians, non-Christians, all
  people of good will everywhere. The Holy Spirit is at work
  among us.

Index

DATE DUE			

HIGHSMITH 45-220